IMPACT YOUR WORLD

TO THE
ENDS OF THE EARTH

CHURCHES FULFILLING THE GREAT COMMISSION

JERRY RANKIN

LifeWay Press®
Nashville, Tennessee

Published by LifeWay Press®
© 2006 International Mission Board, SBC

ISBN 1-4158-3532-2

This book is the resource for course CG-1199 in the subject area Missions
in the Christian Growth Study Plan.

Dewey Decimal classification: 266.023
Subject heading: FOREIGN MISSIONS \ EVANGELISTIC WORK

To order additional copies of this resource, write to LifeWay Church Resources
Customer Service; One LifeWay Plaza; Nashville, TN 37234-0113;
fax (615) 251-5933; phone toll free (800) 458-2772;
order online at *www.lifeway.com;* or visit the LifeWay Christian Store serving you.

Printed in the United States of America

Leadership and Adult Publishing
LifeWay Church Resources
One LifeWay Plaza
Nashville, TN 37234-0175

CONTENTS

Meet the Author

Jerry Rankin is the president of the International Mission Board of the Southern Baptist Convention in Richmond, Virginia. A Mississippi native, Rankin earned a bachelor-of-arts degree from Mississippi College and a master-of-divinity degree from Southwestern Baptist Theological Seminary. He and his wife, Bobbye, spent 23 years as missionaries in Asia before he became the president of the International Mission Board in 1993. Today he leads the board with a vision of missionaries, churches, and volunteers partnering to take the gospel to all peoples.

Prior to becoming a missionary, Rankin served as the pastor of Sadler Baptist Church in Sadler, Texas; the youth director and associate pastor of Sagamore Hill Baptist Church in Fort Worth, Texas; and the Baptist Student Union director and Bible instructor at Grayson County Junior College in Denison, Texas. Rankin is the co-author of *Lives Given, Not Taken: 21st-Century Southern Baptist Martyrs* and the author of *A Journey of Faith and Sacrifice: Retracing the Steps of Lottie Moon.*

The Rankins have two children, both of whom have served with their families as missionaries, and six grandchildren.

ABOUT THIS STUDY

All of us want to leave a legacy for our family, our friends, and our church. We want our lives to make a lasting impact for God's kingdom, but we are not sure how to accomplish this goal. Most of us don't consider ourselves missionaries; instead, we work in offices, factories, farms, schools, homes, and many other places. Can God really use us to reach the world for Christ?

The fact is that every Southern Baptist can be involved in ongoing missions. *To the Ends of the Earth* is a study in the Impact Your World series, which was written by the International Mission Board (IMB) of the Southern Baptist Convention. In this study you will learn how the IMB mobilizes Southern Baptists to reach the ends of the earth with the good news of Jesus Christ and how you and your church can be a part of the IMB's global mission strategy.

When we read statistics about the lostness of the world, the numbers are staggering. Twenty-five percent of the world's population—1.56 billion people—are nonbelievers with little or no access to the gospel. An additional 2.64 billion people are nonbelievers with only limited access to the gospel. Evangelical Christians, composing only 10 percent of the world's population, are vastly outnumbered by those who have never heard the truth of God's Word. Persecution of Christians is at an all-time high, and we are rapidly losing ground to world religions that do not allow Christians to witness openly or even conduct church services.

In a time when so many need to hear the truth of Jesus Christ, missions cannot be delegated to career missionaries. Each believer, as an ambassador of Christ, is responsible for carrying the gospel to the ends of the earth. Church members need to pray for and financially support the cause of winning the lost, but they also need to understand and commit themselves to their individual part in this effort. *To the Ends of the Earth* will help you discover God's specific assignment for you, whether you are training to go on a mission trip, being equipped to serve on your church's missions team, or participating in a study group that wants to learn how to reach the ends of the earth with the gospel.

Southern Baptists are fortunate to have a missionary-sending entity. The IMB enlists, trains, sends, and provides support for more than five thousand missionaries overseas. Joining the IMB in strategizing our involvement in world missions will enable us to reach the world's people groups. It won't be done by each of us going in a different direction. Collectively, we 16 million Southern Baptists in churches, associations, states, and other organizations can plan together to reach this world for Christ. That is the purpose of the Impact Your World series: to help you and your church find your place in this mammoth task before us.

The time is now. The opportunity is present. Let's take Jesus' challenge to heart and respond to His command to take the gospel to the ends of the earth (see Acts 1:8).

Week 1
DISCOVERING GOD'S KINGDOM PURPOSE

VERSES TO REMEMBER

" 'Go, therefore, and make disciples of all nations,
baptizing them in the name of the Father and of the
Son and of the Holy Spirit, teaching them to observe
everything I have commanded you. And remember,
I am with you always, to the end of the age.' "

MATTHEW 28:19-20

As new missionaries in Uruguay, we were on a semideserted stretch of highway in San Jose de Mayo, Uruguay, on our way home from church on a Saturday night. One missionary said, "If you look out that way, you can see a glow on the horizon. That's the city of Buenos Aires! And over there is Montevideo!" I was amazed that I could see the lights of two major cities in two different countries! Even more amazing, in the night sky I could see another glow.

The missionary commented, "We can see more of the Milky Way from the Southern Hemisphere." Surrounded by the darkness, the city lights were bright, but the Milky Way was radiant! I suddenly felt small and insignificant. Yet God reminded me that He led us to reflect His light and love to a dark world. I want to shine like those lights, like those stars. I want to shine before people so they can praise my Father in heaven. Even a small light can penetrate the darkness.[1]—K. C., SOUTH AMERICA

The purpose and vision of the International Mission Board (IMB) of the Southern Baptist Convention were given to us by Jesus in what has been known as the Great Commission, Matthew 28:19-20. Our task is to bring people from all nations to saving faith in Jesus Christ. However, the mission task encompasses every believer in every nation. This means that you and your church are a significant part of God's plan. As you read, look for ways to work with the IMB so that God's vision is accomplished.

DAY 1
GOD'S KINGDOM REIGN IN OUR LIVES

Throughout the Bible we read of a coming kingdom of God in which every tongue will confess Him as Lord and every knee will bow in humble submission to His power and authority. The Old Testament tells how God chose a people to be His possession and commissioned Israel to declare His glory to the pagans around them in the promised land.

Read Exodus 19:5-6. In your own words write (1) God's covenant promise to Israel and (2) Israel's responsibility.

1. _____

2. _____

Kingdom of God: *God's reign over each believer's life now and when Jesus comes to establish the new kingdom and the new earth*

OUR KINGDOM RESPONSIBILITY

When Jesus came, He announced the arrival of the kingdom, which would be purchased by His own blood on the cross. He commanded His followers to proclaim the gospel of the kingdom and to make disciples of all nations. In fact, in Matthew 24:14 He said, " 'The good news of the kingdom will be proclaimed in all the world as a testimony to all nations. And then the end will come.' " All who come to Jesus Christ in personal repentance and faith become a part of that kingdom. And as a kingdom people, we are to be the instruments for extending His kingdom among all peoples.

How does that happen? The kingdom grows as we acknowledge the lordship of Christ and allow Him to reign in our lives. People glorify God when they recognize His authority, obey His will, and live according to His Word.

Jesus spoke of the kingdom as leaven or yeast, small and practically unseen but permeating a whole loaf of bread. That is how we are to be in society—making an impact for righteousness in our families, communities, society, and nation. Jesus also described the kingdom as a mustard seed, the smallest in the garden, which grows into a large tree.

Match the verse or verses on the left with Jesus' description of the kingdom.

___ 1. Matthew 13:31-32   a. The kingdom is within believers. We are kingdom citizens.

___ 2. Matthew 13:33   b. As a kingdom people, we are to extend God's kingdom to all nations.

___ 3. Luke 17:21   c. The kingdom permeates a whole society through a few faithful followers.

___ 4. Matthew 28:19-20   d. Although small now, the kingdom will reach every people group.

The kingdom, which began with Jesus and His small band of disciples, will include citizens from every tribe, language, culture, and nation. Therefore, we as a kingdom people are to actively and deliberately extend the kingdom through our witness and obedience to Christ. Christian organizations, denominations, and mission agencies don't extend the kingdom. Only a massive grassroots force of believers functioning as the body of Christ in the world can accomplish Christ's command. And then only the Holy Spirit's presence in each believer can supply the power to grow the kingdom. The kingdom grows quantitatively, qualitatively, and geographically.

Mark these sentences as true (T) or false (F).

___ The kingdom grows quantitatively as new believers come into the kingdom daily.

___ The kingdom grows qualitatively by using only the best preachers.

___ The kingdom grows geographically as we take the gospel to each lost people group in the most remote parts of the earth.

___ Being a kingdom citizen qualifies each believer to spread the gospel.

Churches are not left to extend the kingdom alone. The role of the denomination at every level should be to help churches by facilitating, equipping, and enabling them to fulfill God's purpose. The Southern Baptist Convention has adopted a vision called Empowering Kingdom Growth. This vision is greater than church or denominational growth. It is bigger than our programs. It is a God-sized vision for impacting our world for Jesus Christ. Every entity—whether an association, a state convention, or a mission agency—exists only to disciple, equip, and enable God's people to fulfill the Great Commission.

> **The Great Commission:** *Jesus' command in Matthew 28:19-20: " 'Go, therefore, and make disciples of all nations, baptizing them in the name of the Father and of the Son and of the Holy Spirit, teaching them to observe everything I have commanded you. And remember, I am with you always, to the end of the age.' "*

> **Empowering Kingdom Growth:** *An initiative that calls Southern Baptists to renew their passion for the Lord Jesus and the reign of His kingdom in their hearts, families, and churches, from which God can forge a spiritual movement marked by holy living, sacrificial service, and global witness*

HOW THE KINGDOM GROWS

Following His death and resurrection, Jesus gave His followers a formula for growing His kingdom. In Acts 1:8 Jesus explained that His followers were to start by planting the gospel in Jerusalem, where they lived. They were to expand from that small mustard seed to permeate the surrounding province of Judea. Then they were to extend the kingdom cross-culturally to Samaria and from there to the most remote corners of the earth.

Our denomination is uniquely organized to facilitate that very pattern of kingdom growth. The cutting-edge witness and building blocks of the kingdom are local churches. Associations have been organized by cooperating local churches to more effectively reach their cities (Jerusalem). State conventions exist to mobilize the efforts of churches collectively to make an impact on their states (Judea). The Southern Baptist Convention has organized the North American Mission Board to coordinate and empower churches to reach out beyond their own communities cross-culturally and geographically to extend the kingdom throughout the United States and Canada (Samaria). And the IMB exists to mobilize, facilitate, and enable every believer, every church, and every denominational partnership to function in a way that results in kingdom growth to the ends of the earth.

Acts 1:8 mentions four geographic areas in which the church is to witness. In the first column list the geographic area that corresponds to where you live. In the second column list the Southern Baptist entity that helps local churches fulfill their witness in that area.

Jerusalem: _____ _____

Judea: _____ _____

Samaria: _____ _____

Ends of the earth: _____ _____

DAY 2
MOTIVATION FOR KINGDOM GROWTH

To understand lostness, we don't need a parade of missionaries coming to our churches. We see lostness every day on television newscasts and in the headlines of our newspapers. We see live video feeds of terrorists and suicide bombers as they seek to destroy lives. We watch masses of devotees bowing in response to the call to prayer, affirming their allegiance to Allah and Mohammed as his prophet. We witness the despair of victims of the genocide spawned by ethnic conflicts. But do we realize that Jesus is the answer to a world in need? He is the light for a world in spiritual darkness, the hope for multitudes in despair.

OUR MANDATE AND OUR RESPONSE

The needs of a lost world should motivate us to become involved in extending the kingdom of God, but we are seldom motivated by needs alone. Every Christian and every church should be conscientious about obeying our Lord's command. He clearly told us to " 'make disciples of all nations' " (Matt. 28:19), " 'to preach the gospel to the whole creation' " (Mark 16:15), and " 'to be My witnesses ... to the ends of the earth' " (Acts 1:8).

We rationalize away Jesus' mandate, which was meant for the church and all of God's people, by assuming it applies only to a few elite Christians who are called as missionaries. Most believers pursue their own plans with no responsibility for those who desperately need to hear the good news of Jesus. Many give financially to supply the mission agencies' needs so that these entities can carry out the Great Commission on their behalf. Others read about missions and pray for missionaries but never tell anyone the gospel message.

Mission: *God's purpose to reach and redeem the world*

Missions: *Christians' activity to fulfill God's redemptive mission*

Southern Baptists take pride in having more than five thousand international missionaries. But that number represents less than $3/10$ of 1 percent of our church members. Does God choose only one of every three thousand faithful church members to go and witness to 95 percent of the world's population? Is it enough for the rest of us to live contentedly among the remaining 5 percent of the population who have abundant opportunities to hear the gospel?

"The Great Commission is sufficient authority, but it is not sufficient motive. It is not the imperative of an external command that sends us after the lost, it is the impulse of an indwelling presence!"[2]
—J. E. CONANT

One would think our Lord's mandate and desire would motivate us to go. But only as we enter a relationship with God that becomes so intimate that we feel His heartbeat will we be compelled to witness to the lost around us and to go to the ends of the earth. Only when we are compelled by God's passion to reach a lost world will we have a vision of joining God on mission and taking responsibility for advancing kingdom growth.

King David had a passion for building the temple, a house of God among His people. Psalm 132:3-5 expresses his passion:

> *I will not enter my house or get into my bed,*
> *I will not allow my eyes to sleep*
> *or my eyelids to slumber*
> *until I find a place for the Lord,*
> *a dwelling for the Mighty One of Jacob.*

We must not rest, indulge in personal comforts, or be diverted from finding a dwelling place for God among the Tripera, the Tuareg, the Baluchi, the Karalkapak, and all other people groups. That must be the passion and vision that motivate us to reach the lost.

Passion: *Intense emotion, conviction, or devotion that compels action*

SHARING GOD'S PASSION

Read Isaiah 6:1-8. Check the following statements that are correct.
❑ 1. God personally issued a call to Isaiah.
❑ 2. Isaiah took the initiative to offer himself to go.
❑ 3. God's call was for anyone who would hear and respond to His appeal.
❑ 4. God sought someone to represent Him to reach His people.
❑ 5. Isaiah was coerced and obligated, contrary to his own desires.
❑ 6. Isaiah was sensitive to God's voice because he had come into God's presence.

Why did Isaiah sense God's heart for a lost world and respond with a willingness to go? God did not single out Isaiah, calling him to go to a people in darkness. No, the call was generic, not personal. Isaiah heard God saying:

> *Who should I send?*
> *Who will go for Us? (Isa. 6:8).*

He didn't wait for God to tap him on the shoulder and say, "You're the one." Isaiah took the initiative and invited God to send him. In essence he said, "Lord, if You need someone to go to people in darkness, here I am. Let me be the one to go."

Why did Isaiah hear God's heart for the people and respond with a submissive spirit? We read in the earlier verses of Isaiah 6 that he had a vision of God high and exalted. When Isaiah came into God's presence, he recognized God's claim on his life. Having entered an intimate relationship with God, Isaiah felt and shared the passion of God's heart. The motivation for our involvement in God's kingdom plan will not come from denominational programs and church promotion. Putting a guilt trip on people will not produce kingdom growth. The kingdom grows when an intimate relationship with God results in our being filled with His passion for all peoples.

Occasionally, someone asks me, "What is the passion of your life?" I can readily articulate my sense of purpose or what I perceive to be God's will for my life. I can talk about my personal desires, dreams, and visions. But this question always gives me pause. I am passionate about my family, especially my grandchildren. Occasionally, I have become quite passionate in rooting for a favorite team at a sporting event. I have been known to express a passion for our mission task. But do these represent the passion of my life?

Circle what you feel passionate about.

Sports   Politics   Your family   The suffering of the homeless

The right to life   God's ideal for marriage   Your job   Entertainment

Others: _____

_____

How would an observer know about your passion for these concerns?

_____

_____

Is there a compelling force that fills you with emotion, drives your decisions, focuses your attention, energizes your actions, motivates your behavior toward a desired accomplishment, and makes you rejoice when it occurs? God's passion is for all the peoples of the earth to know and praise Him. He has a passion to be exalted among the nations. Should not God's passion be ours as well? Is there anything other than God's glory among the nations that is worthy of our devotion? Jesus' passion for the nations led Him to leave the glory of heaven to provide redemption for a lost world. We will be motivated to obey His mandate only when we have such an intimate relationship with God that we know His heart and share His passion.

Are you open to responding as Isaiah did to God's question? Pray, asking God to open your heart to feel His heartbeat for the lost.

DAY 3
EXTENDING THE KINGDOM TO ALL PEOPLES

We often quote what may be the most familiar verse in the Bible: "'God loved the world in this way: He gave His One and Only Son, so that everyone who believes in Him will not perish but have eternal life'" (John 3:16). That world is not just the world of our shopping malls, manicured lawns, stylish homes, and well-appointed offices. It includes people in dusty, remote villages in Africa, where people are held in bondage to their charms and fetishes and more than six thousand die of AIDS every day. It includes more than one billion people in India, most of whom bow before lifeless Hindu idols in a futile search for blessings and enlightenment. It includes multitudes of Muslims across northern Africa, the Middle East, and central Asia who declare their belief in Allah and Mohammed as his prophet in a fatalistic faith that offers no hope and assurance.

AN OUTWARD FOCUS

A kingdom perspective is not self-centered; it has an outward focus. God has brought us into a relationship with Him as His people to facilitate building His kingdom through evangelism, discipleship, and missions. We tend to have a very egocentric theology. If most Christians were asked why Jesus died on the cross, they would reply, "To save me from my sin." That is correct; He died for all. When we come to Jesus in repentance and faith, His death on the cross is for the penalty of our sin, and we are saved through faith. But note the answer to this question in the words of Jesus Himself: "'This is what is written: the Messiah would suffer and rise from the dead the third day, and repentance for forgiveness of sins would be proclaimed in His name to all the nations, beginning at Jerusalem'" (Luke 24:46-47).

> Based on Luke 24:46-47, what was the purpose of Jesus' death?
> Underline the best answer.
> • He died and rose to glorify God.
> • He died and rose to save individuals from their sin.
> • He died and rose as a message of salvation for all nations and people.
> • He died and rose to forgive me of my sins.

Those nations for whom Jesus died are not the geographic, political units we know on our maps today as countries. They represent the multiplicity of culturally diverse language and ethnic people groups throughout the world. Most faithful Southern Baptists know and can quote John 3:16. In addition, they must know and obey what we call the Great Commission in Matthew 28:19-20: "'All authority has been given to Me in heaven and on earth. Go, therefore, and make disciples of all nations, baptizing them in the name of the Father and of the Son and of the Holy Spirit, teaching them to observe everything I have commanded you. And remember, I am with you always, to the end of the age.'" Jesus' words are translated *all nations* in the original Greek, or *panta ta ethne*, which literally means *all the peoples*.

> **People group/people:** *A group of individuals, frequently speaking the same language, who share a self-identity and worldview. Strategically, a people group is the largest group through which the gospel can flow without encountering a significant barrier.*

Jesus was saying something more than evangelizing all people, that is, all of the individuals in the world, even though that is His desire and would bring glory to Him. The expression He used, *ethne* or *ethnos,* is the same as our word *ethnic,* distinct cultural and racial characteristics that distinguish some people from others. Jesus commissioned His disciples—and that includes us today—to bring into the kingdom of God and make disciples—Christlike followers—of every ethnic, cultural, and language group in the world.

Some tend to dilute the Great Commission to refer to whatever we do in witnessing, evangelism, and ministry. However, the only active verb in our Lord's command is *make;* all other verbs—*going, baptizing, teaching*—are participles. The imperative verb *make disciples* is grammatically a transitive verb, meaning it requires an object. In our English translations *disciples* appears to be the object of the verb *make.* In Greek, however, the object is *all peoples.* So the object of the verb is make *all peoples.* The parallel passage in Acts 1:8 makes that responsibility clear, whether the people group, language, and culture are in Jerusalem, in Judea, in Samaria, or at the ends of the earth.

OVERCOMING BARRIERS

Only recently has the IMB come to understand our Great Commission task in terms of the peoples of the world. We once thought that sending missionaries to any given country would eventually evangelize an entire nation. Consider Yugoslavia as an example. Events in recent years have shown us that the nation once called Yugoslavia was not really a cohesive, homogeneous country but consisted of Serbs, Bosnians, Croats, Slovenians, Kosovars, Macedonians, and other people groups. Each had different languages and cultural identities. Conflicts in the region demonstrated that evidently, these people did not especially like one another.

If one of these people groups could be penetrated with the gospel, it would not necessarily spread to other groups who speak different languages and have antagonistic relationships. Evangelism cannot accomplish its purpose by just approaching all of these people groups as Yugoslavians. A similar situation exists in Pakistan. We are not sent to evangelize Pakistan but to make disciples—followers of Christ—among the Baluchi, the Punjabi, the Sindhi, the Pashto, and other people groups who occupy the country.

We have discovered that the world is not a pancake but a waffle. When you pour syrup on a pancake, the syrup flows all over the smooth, round surface. If you want syrup all over your waffle, you very deliberately have to pour it in each little square. The world is not a monolithic collection of homogeneous peoples shaped like a pancake. It contains more than 12,000 diverse languages, tribes, and ethnic identities. Like the ridges on a waffle, barriers keep the gospel from flowing cross-culturally. These barriers are represented in the names of nations, languages, and culture.

An obvious barrier is language. A research database known as ROPAL (Registry of Peoples and Languages) identifies 6,809 distinct languages. Only 2,322 of them have some portion of Scripture; fewer than 1,000 have the full Bible in their language. Many of these languages are used in oral cultures, and speakers could not read from the Bible even if one were available in their language. For this reason illiteracy is another barrier that resists traditional methods of evangelism and discipleship.

> Recall the story of the tower of Babel in Genesis 11:1-9. Why did God confuse the languages of these people? Check one or more reasons.
> ❏ Some languages were too hard to understand.
> ❏ The people had become arrogant and disobedient.
> ❏ The people would not be able to build the tower if they could not understand one another.
> ❏ The tower would have been unsafe, and many would have died.

All believers will once again have a common language when Jesus comes to reestablish His new kingdom and new earth.

Another barrier to the gospel is geography. Many people groups who have never heard the gospel are isolated in places where missionaries have never been allowed, primarily in the Muslim world or in former Communist countries—totalitarian governments that prohibit religious freedom. No churches and believers are present in their midst to tell them about Jesus. But whatever the distinction—whether language, geographic location, or ethnicity—

cultural identity is a matter of "us" and "them," those who belong due to a common language, values, and relationships and those who are outsiders.

Write each of the following words in the appropriate column to identify it as a nation, language, or people group.

Nigeria, Spanish, Korea, Han Chinese, Mandarin, Navajo, Brazil, K'etchi, Swahili, India, Egyptian, Arabic, Hindi, Iraq, Tamil

Nation	Language	People Group
_____	_____	_____
_____	_____	_____
_____	_____	_____
_____	_____	_____
_____	_____	_____

DAY 4
OUR RESPONSIBILITY FOR KINGDOM GROWTH

Because of accelerating evangelistic efforts in recent years, we are told that approximately 10 percent of the world's population—around 600 million—is composed of born-again believers. When we think that 1 of every 10 people has come to saving faith in Jesus Christ, the task of reaching everyone seems achievable; all it would take is every Christian winning 9 others. However, the problem is a matter of proportion. Unfortunately, 95 percent of those believers are clumped together in America and other places where the church has been established. Meanwhile, hundreds of people groups, some numbering in the millions, have yet to hear the name of Jesus. More than two thousand years after Jesus sent His followers to make disciples of all nations, researchers estimate that 1.65 billion people have no access to the gospel.

AN UNMET GOAL

In recent years significant progress has been made in taking the gospel to all peoples. In 1995 the A.D. 2000 and Beyond organization sponsored a Global Consultation on World Evangelization in Seoul, South Korea. More than 4,000 people from 180 countries gathered specifically to discuss how the Great Commission could be completed by the year 2000. The goal was to plant a church in every people group in the world. Although we obviously did not meet this auspicious goal, the impact of the consultation accelerated global mission efforts. At that time researchers reported 2,161 ethnic-linguistic people groups that had not been touched by the gospel. Many of them had populations in the millions. These people groups represented a cumulative population of 1.68 billion people who had not yet even heard the name of Jesus.

By 2004 that number of people groups had been reduced to fewer than 300, mostly smaller micro-people groups. Mission agencies have adjusted priorities and refocused resources; however, almost 6,525 people groups—as many as 3.4 billion people—remain less than 2 percent evangelized and are identified as unreached. Although some churches exist in their countries and Christian materials are available in their languages, most of the people do not have access to a personal Christian witness.

Elsewhere, in countries where missionaries have been able to proclaim the gospel through Christian media and literature and readily available Bibles, churches have grown to reach up to 10 percent or more of the population. However, 2 billion people in these countries are adherents of other religions and have not in any way declared their faith in Jesus Christ.

Micro-people group: *A people group with a relatively small population*

The Status of Global Evangelization Model

		Status	Description
Unreached People Groups	Last Frontier	0	No evangelical Christians or churches No access to major evangelical print, audiovisual, or human resources
		1	Less than 2% evangelical. Some evangelical resources available but no active church planting within past two years
		2	Less than 2% evangelical. Initial (localized) church planting within past two years
		3	Less than 2% evangelical. Widespread church planting within past two years
		4	Greater than or equal to 2% evangelical
		5	Greater than or equal to 5% evangelical
		6	Greater than or equal to 10% evangelical
		7	Unknown

OUR MISSION

Certainly, God wants us to witness where we live and minister to the people around us, but if we don't carry the gospel to those who have never heard, who will? Because God has given us the privilege of knowing Him, we have a responsibility to share that with which we have been entrusted—the light of the gospel. We are to keep sharing until news of God's salvation literally reaches every people group to the ends of the earth.

IMB Vision Statement

We will lead Southern Baptists to be on mission with God to bring
all the peoples of the world to saving faith in Jesus Christ.

Read Genesis 12:3. What did God promise in His call to Abraham?

I will make your name _____, and you will be a _____.

Read Psalm 67:1-2. For what purpose should God's people expect Him

to bless and be gracious to them? _____

Why should we expect God to bless us and prosper our church programs if the purpose is not for the sake of proclaiming His salvation among the nations, the peoples who live around us, and to the ends of the earth? God desires all peoples to know Him and praise Him. He is worthy of all honor and glory and praise, but He is being deprived of the praise of the people groups who do not yet know Him and have not yet come to faith in Jesus Christ. Psalm 100 begins, "Shout triumphantly to the Lord, all the earth." Psalm 96:1 says, "Sing to the Lord, all the earth." The ultimate objective is for all lands and all the earth to praise His name. How can that be accomplished?

What are God's people told to do in Psalm 96:3?

Declare His g_____ and His wonderful w_____ among

_____ _____.

Read Isaiah 49:6. How did God express our task among other peoples?

We are to be a l_____ for the nations and God's salvation to _____

_____ _____ _____ _____.

DAY 5
A VISION FOR KINGDOM GROWTH

The IMB's methods are based on the foundational strategies of prayer and church planting, both of which are essential components of kingdom growth. All methods must begin with a vision—sharing God's vision—of all peoples coming to saving faith in Jesus Christ.

> We are told about the power of the gospel in Romans 10:13-14: "Everyone who calls on the name of the Lord will be saved." Fill in the blanks with the missing words in the rest of the passage.
>
> "How can they _____ on Him in whom they have not _____? And how can they_____ without a preacher? And how can they preach unless they are _____?" (Rom. 10:14).

OUR VISION

The word *vision* comes from the Latin word *spiare,* which means *to breathe* or *to inspire and energize.* Without a vision inspiring us, driving us, and energizing us, we will tend to flounder and lose energy and resources, responding to pressures and going in multiple directions without really getting anywhere. The IMB has always been guided by strategies for evangelizing a lost world. But a strategy is only as good as the vision that drives it.

> **Vision:** *A clear, intentional goal that drives a ministry and provides direction for its priorities and actions*

A vision that results in kingdom growth emerges from a heartfelt conviction about God's power to change lives and spontaneously spread His gospel. God is at work and is calling us to join Him to reach all peoples. Without a vision, church programs and mission strategies can go in any direction. Organizations can define their purposes and identify their objectives and goals, but a vision or an image of the future keeps them focused and on track. A vision keeps us from being diverted to secondary or trivial activities. A vision enables an individual, a church, and a denomination to be effective in fulfilling God's kingdom purpose.

"There is no more powerful engine driving an organization toward excellence and long-range success than an attractive, worthwhile, and achievable vision of the future."[3]
—BURT NANUS

What vision do you have for your life? _____

_____

What is your vision for your church? _____

_____

What is God's vision for the world? _____

_____

Several years ago the IMB began to realize that we needed to make significant changes in order to fulfill our vision of leading Southern Baptists to be on mission with God. We asked ourselves, *How are we going to bring all peoples of the world to saving faith in Jesus Christ?* Here are some of the changes we made.

We realized that we could not be dependent on the limited resources of the IMB but needed to mobilize the resources of Southern Baptists. Even five thousand God-called, trained, and equipped missionaries who were passionately devoted to evangelism could not touch the whole world. We would have to double the number of missionaries just to have one person assigned to each people group. We realized that God had raised up 16 million Southern Baptists—43,000 churches; 1,200 associations; and 40 state conventions, plus multiple colleges, seminaries, and other entities—all with the potential to make an impact on a lost world. When we envisioned the potential of mobilizing and involving our denomination for the purpose to which God had called us as His people, the vision of global evangelism became achievable.

God has blessed and prospered Southern Baptists in numbers and resources not to take pride in being a great denomination but to be His people on mission to reach a lost world.

We realized that we could no longer take pride in annual statistical growth but had to measure success and progress only by global impact. We have always embraced strategic planning. Globally, each region and every local missionary had goals for baptisms, membership growth, and planting churches. Every year we would pat ourselves on the back when baptisms increased, a few more churches were planted than in the previous year, and the number of missionaries increased. We were guilty of what Paul described in 2 Corinthians 10:12: "Measuring themselves by themselves and comparing themselves to themselves." But significance is not about what we do one year compared to the past year. Success is not determined by how big we are compared to previous years.

The only measure of success is whether we are making an impact on a lost world. Success is determined by whether we make progress in taking the gospel to every tribe, language, and nation. That is the vision of God's kingdom.

We realized that our global mission task could not be driven by human-sized goals but must be driven by a God-sized vision. At that time our objectives and strategic planning seldom reflected projections beyond what we realistically felt could be accomplished. We tended to limit our vision by what had been done in the past. Now we know that we are not capable of reaching the whole world, but if that is God's purpose and plan, then our vision can be no less. We cannot settle for simply extending our witness to a few more countries or engaging an additional number of unreached people groups. We cannot be satisfied with record numbers of baptisms among established churches where the gospel was already being proclaimed. God's passion and heart are for all peoples. Our strategies, organization, personnel deployment, and mobilization efforts must be focused and driven by a God-sized vision, which is nothing less than seeing all peoples of the world come to saving faith in Jesus Christ!

> **Unreached people group:** *A people group composed of less than 2 percent evangelical Christians*

IMPLEMENTING OUR VISION

It became evident that implementing these changes in our perspective had to be accompanied by three paradigm shifts:

- Personalization instead of generic support
- Partnership instead of exclusive control
- Passion as the motivation instead of program promotion

Southern Baptists have always been faithful to support our missionaries. We take pride in sending out more than five thousand missionaries, but we do not know them or know what they are doing, and most missionaries never hear from Southern Baptist church members. Churches are increasingly supporting parachurch and independent mission organizations. No wonder church-based allocations to the Cooperative Program, Southern Baptists' plan for denominational funding, continue to diminish.

The IMB is seeking ways to give churches personal ownership of the mission task and opportunities to be involved as partners with missionaries in reaching people groups around the world. But the vision will be driven only by a passion for God's kingdom task of reaching a lost world, not by the promotion of the IMB and our denominational programs.

The Great Commission was not given to the IMB but to every church, every believer, and every denominational entity. The IMB's task as a denominational mission agency is not to be the proxy representative for Southern Baptist mission efforts but to channel the support, facilitate the involvement, and mobilize the resources. Our responsibility and commitment are to enable and empower God's people through a vision that is characterized by God's power and compelled by God's passion.

Write your understanding of the IMB's vision to lead Southern Baptists as expressed in the following phrases. What is meant by each phrase?

Personalization instead of generic support: _____

_____

Partnership instead of exclusive control: _____

_____

Passion instead of program promotion: _____

_____

How did God express His vision for missions in Revelation 7:9? _____

_____

1. Adapted from *Voices of the Faithful,* comp. Kim P. Davis (Brentwood, TN: Integrity Publishers, 2005), 18.
2. J. E. Conant, *Every-Member Evangelism* (New York: Harper & Brothers, 1922), 122–23.
3. Burt Nanus, *Visionary Leadership* (Jossey-Bass, 1992), 3.

WEEK 2

GROWING GOD'S KINGDOM
THROUGH MISSIONS

VERSE TO REMEMBER

"The Lord does not delay His promise, as some
understand delay, but is patient with you, not wanting
any to perish, but all to come to repentance."
2 Peter 3:9

Sydney, a man in India, is the only believer in his family. His parents, devout Jat Sikhs, have threatened him, beaten him, emotionally blackmailed him, and disinherited him to try to convince him to leave his faith. His father even offered him a large sum of money to return to Sikhism. Sydney chose to stay with Jesus. He has a passion to see God glorified among the Jat Sikhs. To be more strategic in sharing the gospel and planting churches, he recently moved to an area where many Jat Sikhs live. He believes that with time even his parents can come to Jesus.[1]

In Jesus' parables about lostness in Luke 15, He told the stories of a lost sheep, coin, and son. In each case the lost was found, with much rejoicing. Does God care about lost sinners? Does He rejoice when one of them joins His family? In this week's study you will learn how you and your church can implement evangelistic strategies to provide all people an opportunity to respond to Christ's claims as Savior in their own cultural contexts.

DAY 1
THE CHALLENGE OF LOSTNESS

IMB Basic Belief

Jesus Christ is God's only provision for salvation, and people without personal faith in Him are lost and will spend eternity in hell.

In previous generations Christians were not branded as intolerant because of their belief that Jesus Christ is God's only provision for salvation and that people without personal faith in Him are lost and will spend eternity in hell. However, postmodern influences have eroded the conviction of many that only one way leads to God. In its place we live in a world without Christ and with the consequences of sin. Yet hell is real, and eternity is long. Hell remains the destiny of everlasting, irreversible torment once a nonbeliever passes from this earthly life.

How are those without Christ described in the following verses?

Romans 3:23: They have _____ .

Ephesians 2:1-2: They are _____ .

Whether someone has heard and rejected the gospel or has never had an opportunity to hear of God's provision for salvation, the destiny is the same. Obviously, if this statement were not true, we would have no basis for missions. Missions is all about lostness. Missions is not simply a matter of statistical growth—tallying the number of missionaries sent out or the professions of faith in a given year. Missions proclaims the gospel and makes it accessible to all peoples of the world so that those in darkness can come to the Light of the world.

Lostness: *The condition of people who do not have personal faith in Christ and face separation from God for all eternity as the consequence of their sin*

A WORLD WITHOUT CHRIST

Across a relatively evangelized African continent, pockets of darkness remain where fetishes and witch doctors hold people in bondage to ancient fears and superstitions. Faster than a

Christian witness can be shared, the haunting specter of AIDS claims more than six thousand lives a day, decimating the wage earners of society and leaving millions of orphans. Social deterioration, political instability, and ethnic warfare run rampant throughout Africa, leaving the quality of life in shambles. Crime, illiteracy, and joblessness weave a pall of hopelessness over the people. Sadder still is the hopelessness beyond this life for masses of people. A total of 1,521 unreached people groups south of the Sahara do not know Jesus.

> How does this picture of Africans affect your concern for their salvation?
> ❑ Somewhat concerned   ❑ Concerned   ❑ Very concerned
>
> What actions are you willing to take to reach the African continent for Christ?
> ❑ I will pray and give to missions.
> ❑ I will volunteer to go on a mission trip to Africa.
> ❑ God has not shown me how to help.
> ❑ We have lost people in our neighborhood. Why should I go to Africa?
> ❑ I will learn about possible actions I could take to help.
>
> Read Romans 10:1 below. Underline the way Paul felt about nonbelievers.
> "My heart's desire and prayer to God concerning them is for their salvation!"

I'll never forget my first trip to Russia soon after the fall of Communism. Our group felt a sense of disbelief as we walked through Red Square, saw the grandeur of historical landmarks, and attended the ballet *Swan Lake* in Moscow's Hall of Congress. But what I remember most is the lingering impression of oppressiveness, the sullen demeanor of the people, and the drabness of our surroundings. I remember our missionaries living in small, cramped apartments; trying to relate to suspicious neighbors; and coping with limited consumer goods and long, cold winters to share the Light of the world with those so long deprived of religious freedom.

A subsequent trip to India reinforced the intensity of how dark the world can be without Christ. I arrived in Delhi during the Kumbh Mela festival, the largest religious gathering in the world. Once every three years this three-month event is held at one of the four holy cities on the Ganges River. That year the festival was in Hardiwar, where more than 10 million Hindus gathered to bathe in the waters of the river, believing that act would wash away sin. As we stood on the rooftop of a nearby building gazing on the panorama before us, my heart was broken. As we watched, the massive congestion of humanity scurried about to get into the frigid waters flowing down from the Himalayas. But that scene was only a precursor to the experience a couple of days later when we visited the Kali temple upon our arrival in Calcutta.

In the midst of pungent incense and clanging bells, pilgrims crowded into the temple courtyard. The altar before the black, multiheaded goddess of Calcutta flowed with blood as people brought goats and sacrificed them. Devotees rushed forward, dipping their fingers in the blood and pressing it to their foreheads. They did not know that the blood of calves and goats will not save them. The precious blood of our Lord Jesus Christ cleanses from sin. Idol worship is not just an ancient phenomenon depicted among uneducated and unenlightened pagan tribes in biblical days. It is a reality throughout the world today.

You do not have to go far to see idol worship. Have statues of idols begun to appear in restaurants and stores in your town? ❑ Yes ❑ No
Does your community have a temple? ❑ Yes ❑ No
Does it have a mosque? ❑ Yes ❑ No

A FALSE SECURITY

Some of the greatest barriers to knowing Jesus are not in the Hindu or Muslim world—among animists and unreached peoples—but in places where people think they are Christians. Some researchers consider places like Latin America or western Europe to be evangelized. Although steeples of churches and cathedrals punctuate the skyline of every city and village, the lostness in these places is evident. Although the people have never read the Bible and attend church only for weddings and funerals, their self-identity is "Christian." Their false security creates a smug satisfaction that makes it difficult to penetrate their culture with the claims of Christ.

Though churches abound in Latin America, spiritism has perverted their doctrine and has claimed more adherents than evangelical believers. To travel through Mexico City, with 21.2 million people; Sao Paulo, Brazil, with 19 million; and other cities overwhelms me with the massive challenge of lostness. In some ways South Americans—with their penance before icons, trust in charms, and ritualistic prayers—differ little from Hindu worshipers in India.

However, the response to the gospel in Africa and Latin America has accelerated. The frontiers of Asia are reaping an increasing harvest as a Christian witness sweeps across previously untouched frontiers. But the most foreboding, formidable barrier to kingdom growth remains in the Muslim world across northern Africa, throughout the Middle East, and into central Asia. For centuries the followers of Islam have strengthened their stranglehold on the Arab world and neighboring countries. Restrictive policies have kept any Christian presence to a minimum and have prohibited open witness. The shrill sound of the minarets, calling the people to prayer five times a day, bears testimony of the lostness of multitudes with little chance of hearing of a personal God who loves them and offers grace for salvation. They have a firmly ingrained belief in a fatalistic religion controlled by a punitive God who cannot be known.

Read John 3:18 in your Bible. Can Islam and Christianity both be right?
❑ Yes ❑ No Explain your answer.

_____

What do you feel God is saying to you about the world's lostness?

_____

Christians proclaim a message of hope for those in despair and salvation for those trapped in sin. As His followers extend the witness of God's love to them, we glorify God by making His kingdom known so that He is exalted by all peoples of the world.

DAY 2
DISPELLING THE DARKNESS

Jesus made the contrast clear. He distinguished the truth found in Him alone from that claimed by all other religious and cultural traditions. Jesus could not have affirmed it more strongly than when His argument with the Pharisees reached a peak of confrontation.

Read John 8:12 in your Bible. What claim did Jesus make about Himself?

_____

Who are those who have the light of life? _____

How are those without Christ described? _____

Those who have come to faith in Jesus live in the light of God's truth. They have become part of His eternal kingdom. Those who do not believe in Jesus as Savior and Lord are in darkness. When Jesus quoted the prophet Isaiah in Matthew 4:16, He continued that analogy and put into perspective the global, eternal purpose of His mission to redeem a lost world:

"The people who sat in darkness saw a great light.
And upon those who sat in the region and shadow of death
Light has dawned" (NKJV).

DISPELLING THE DARKNESS

That Light began its unquenchable illumination as the dawn of resurrection morning over-powered the darkness that had enveloped the cross. Generations of missionaries and Christian witnesses have continued to proclaim the Light to those who dwell under the shadow of death in spiritual darkness. Yet two thousand years after the Light arrived, the darkness remains.

How can the darkness be dispelled so that those who dwell in it can have the light of life? The hymn "We've a Story to Tell" expresses the biblical foundations for kingdom growth. That's it! All we really need is the story of the gospel—a story of truth and mercy, a story of peace and light. The message of that story has the power to dispel the darkness. Paul said the gospel "is God's power for salvation to everyone who believes" (Rom. 1:16).

Because the story is being told and many are hearing the gospel for the first time, the chorus of that hymn is becoming a reality:

For the darkness shall turn to dawning,
And the dawning to noonday bright,
And Christ's great kingdom shall come on earth,
The kingdom of love and light.[2]

Because of His love, God allowed the light to shine in our hearts and reveal the mystery of the gospel so that we will pray, we will give, and we will go to a world still in darkness.

Read 2 Corinthians 4:6 below. Underline who brought the Light out of darkness. Circle whom we begin to look like when we shine for God.

"God, who said, 'Light shall shine out of darkness,'—He has shone in our hearts to give the light of the knowledge of God's glory in the face of Jesus Christ" (2 Cor. 4:6).

Can you imagine our Heavenly Father's excitement when you and I came to the light and embraced Jesus Christ as our Savior? He saw the potential of another witness who would faithfully proclaim the Light of the World to the peoples still in darkness. Through your salvation His plan for extending the kingdom to the ends of the earth was at work.

The prophet Isaiah reminded us of the darkness that covers the earth but assured us that the power of light will dispel the darkness:

> *Arise, shine, for your light has come,*
> *And the glory of the Lord shines over you.*
> *For look, darkness covers the earth,*
> *and total darkness the peoples; but the Lord will shine over you,*
> *and His glory will appear over you.*
> *Nations will come to your light (Isa. 60:1-3).*

While traveling in central Asia, I had just completed a tour of Kazakhstan, Kyrgyzstan, Tajikistan, Uzbekistan, and Azerbaijan, newly independent republics that had broken off from the Soviet Union. Centuries of Islamic indoctrination had been brushed with a veneer of atheism from 70 years of Communist domination. As we traveled through country after country, I was thrilled to see evidence of the gospel being sown. Missionary personnel told of widespread spiritual hunger. They gave exciting reports of newly planted churches discipling and training national believers.

On the final night of the journey our regional leadership team and I discussed the 12 million unreached Uighur people who straddled the border of Kazakhstan and China. As we rejoiced in all the peoples who were hearing the gospel, I asked: "How many people groups in these central-Asian republics have been reached with the gospel and churches planted among them?" The reply was 60!

I then asked, "How many people groups have not yet been reached in the region?" The regional leader replied with deep emotion that 300 people groups were still waiting for someone to tell them about Christ. "The most difficult thing about being the regional leader for central Asia," he continued, "is having to decide in our strategic planning, with such limited resources and personnel, which people groups will be deprived of the gospel yet another year." As I flew home the next day, this question burned in my heart: by what criteria should any people be deprived of hearing the gospel?

STILL WAITING

God has opened doors of opportunity that we would never have imagined just a few years ago. Yet people living in darkness, desperate for a message of hope, still wait for someone to come and tell them. God has blessed us so richly. Will we take seriously our obedience to what our Lord Jesus Christ has told us to do about reaching the nations? How will we give account to our Lord for our neglect as we lay before Him our beautiful, well-appointed buildings? As we tell Him of all our church programs that blessed and served the community of the redeemed, how will we justify the little that was given and the few who went to bring the nations and peoples of the world into His kingdom? Many have asked, "Why should anyone hear the gospel twice before everyone has had a chance to hear it once?"

Check those who are responsible for telling others the gospel message.
❑ Preachers   ❑ Gospel singers
❑ Missionaries   ❑ Staff members
❑ Bible-study leaders ❑ Me

I believe God will hold us accountable for every person who dies in sin and goes to hell without ever having an opportunity to hear, understand, and respond to the gospel. God desires for none to perish but for all to come to repentance (see 2 Pet. 3:9). He has committed to us as His followers the task of proclaiming the good news. God will judge His people for a lack of obedience, for our failure to reap the harvest where people are open and responsive. We are not just to witness where we live or where people are responsive. We are to take the gospel to everyone so that God's kingdom will extend to the ends of the earth.

Just as turning on a light switch in a dark room dispels the darkness, so will our witness dispel the darkness among the nations. The light doesn't have to struggle to overcome the dark, for it is the very nature of the light to prevail. But until we are willing to go, in obedience to our Lord and our biblical mission to share the light, people will remain in darkness.

How far are you willing for your light to shine? Place an X on the line.

In my heart   To people in darkness

DAY 3
THE EXCLUSIVITY OF JESUS

Write *T* or *F* beside each statement to identify it as true or false.

_____ 1. All religions are valid ways to find and know God.

_____ 2. It doesn't matter what people choose to believe as long as they are true to their beliefs and follow them with sincerity and integrity.

_____ 3. No religion can claim to have absolute truth about the way to God.

_____ 4. Worshipers in other cultures can be followers of Christ without even knowing it.

_____ 5. The objective of missions is to get people to change their religion.

_____ 6. Faith in Jesus Christ is the only way a person can know God and be saved.

_____ 7. God has chosen to reveal Himself in other cultures through Mohammed, Buddha, and founders of other religions.

_____ 8. If a person has never heard of Jesus or had an opportunity to believe in Him, God in His mercy will provide other ways for that person to be saved.

_____ 9. A person must have heard or read the gospel in order to be saved.

As we become more aware of unreached people groups who have never heard of Jesus, we tend to rationalize their spiritual condition. They are isolated culturally and geographically where there is no church. They have their religious rituals, their gods, and their cultural traditions. Many think that a loving and merciful God would not send them to hell if they died without ever hearing of Jesus. They rationalize that because of their ignorance and sincerity, these people must have another chance to be saved.

That conclusion would be partially correct because God does not condemn them to hell; they are condemned by their sin. Romans 3:23 reads, "All have sinned and fall short of the glory of God," and Romans 6:23 tells us, "The wages of sin is death." Those who never come to repentance and faith in Jesus Christ are condemned by their own sin. Sin separates them from a holy and righteous God. The idea of a noble savage with a pure and sincere heart who serves the gods of his culture is a myth. People everywhere without Christ are sinners with a depraved nature just like ours.

Read Romans 10:1-2 below. Underline the group to whom Paul was referring.

"My heart's desire and prayer to God concerning them is for their salvation! I can testify about them that they have zeal for God, but not according to knowledge."

- Gentiles who were hearing the gospel for the first time
- Savages who were open to the message of the one true God
- The most religious of the Jews, God's chosen nation

Check your answer in Romans 9:3. Paul said that he would be willing to be condemned if by his sacrifice the Israelites could be saved. These were people who worshiped the true and living God and sought to follow His laws but were lost. They did not believe Jesus died for their sins. How much more lost are those who have no knowledge of the truth? The reality of universal sin provides no other alternative for people to be saved than by faith in Jesus Christ.

WHY EVERYONE IS ACCOUNTABLE

Let's suppose that those who have never heard the gospel died without ever knowing the name of Jesus. Then, in His mercy, God made a provision by which they would be saved. If that were true, our most effective mission strategy should be silence. We should determine never to speak Jesus' name again so that someone who has never heard will not hear and subsequently be accountable for his or her sin. But that is not what the Bible tells us. The pages of God's Word are filled with the urgent command to make disciples of all nations, to preach the gospel to every creature, to be witnesses to the ends of the earth. The promise of a Redeemer was given so that all the earth might look to Him and be saved. God would not have gone to the extent of sacrificing His Son if there had been any other way for people to be saved.

Read John 14:6 and fill in the blanks:

"Jesus told him, 'I am the _____, the _____, and the _____. No one comes to the Father except through _____.' "

What did the apostles declare about the way to be saved in Acts 4:12?

" 'There is _____ in no one else, for there is no other _____ under heaven given to people by which we must be saved.' "

We don't have the option of viewing a lost world from any perspective other than that described in God's Word. The Bible reveals Jesus as the only way and hope of salvation. Those who have never come to Him in repentance and faith are lost, whether they have rejected the gospel or have never heard. Those of us who claim to know Christ and to be His followers are not given the option of another way. We, as His people, are to be His witnesses to the ends of the earth. We have a responsibility to proclaim the gospel so that all peoples have the opportunity to hear and respond to God's salvation.

A PLURALISTIC SOCIETY

Over time our once Christian society has become pluralistic. We have befriended Hindu neighbors. We encounter Muslims in shopping malls and Buddhists in restaurants. They all appear to be good citizens with fine families and are considerate of others. Surely, we reason, they are just as saved in the religion they choose to follow as Christians are. They accuse us of being narrow-minded, intolerant, and arrogant for sending missionaries to other religions and cultures and presuming to convert them to our way of life.

Missionaries are often criticized for seeking to proselytize other faiths and for disrupting indigenous cultures. Neither charge is valid. Changing from one religion to another does no good whatsoever, whether as the result of coercion, incentives, or a personal decision of conscience. All religions represent futile human efforts to connect with God. Christianity is a relationship, not a religion. A personal relationship with God comes only through believing in Jesus Christ. Only Christ, in His death on the cross and His resurrection, has removed the barrier of sin, enabling us to be reconciled with a holy and righteous God.

Indigenous: *Originating from within the local context*

We may commend other religions for providing many common elements of ethical teaching and social responsibility; yet none offers assurance of salvation from sin.

> Have you ever witnessed to someone from another culture or religion?
> If so, write about it on a separate sheet of paper and be prepared to relate
> it in your next group session. If not, imagine how the conversation would
> go. What topics might come to the surface? Would you be prepared?

Conviction about Christ's uniqueness is basic to Christian theology. This belief compels us to fulfill our mission of proclaiming Him to all the world. Jesus Christ provides the only way of salvation from sin; only He can reconcile us with a holy and righteous God. This message is truly good news for a lost world, and it must be proclaimed. All peoples deserve to hear it. Our Lord has instructed us to bear witness of this truth everywhere.

> Before you were saved, what was your relationship with God? I was spiritually _____. What was your eternal destiny? I was headed toward a destiny in _____.

> Read Romans 10:9. What did you do to gain eternal life and assurance of salvation from sin?

> _____

> What should others do who are lost in sin and have never accepted the salvation God provided through Jesus Christ?

> _____

DAY 4
EVANGELISM AND DISCIPLESHIP

IMB Basic Purpose
Provide all people an opportunity to hear, understand, and respond to the gospel in their own cultural context

If you are a Southern Baptist, you help support the International Mission Board. That gives you a stake in knowing who we are, what we do, and how effectively we do our work. You may believe or may have heard that our purpose is to convert people overseas, but we cannot convert people. Only the regenerating work of the Holy Spirit can bring someone to faith in Jesus Christ. Our purpose is to provide all people an opportunity to hear, understand, and respond to the gospel in their own cultural context. In response to our witness and proclamation, many will have a genuine experience of being born again.

RELIGION VS. RELATIONSHIP

When people say all religions are the same, they are right. It really doesn't matter which one someone chooses to follow. Teaching religious beliefs and embracing them intellectually mean nothing with regard to salvation. Only a personal, saving relationship with Jesus Christ that comes through repentance and faith can make a difference. That is the power of the gospel.

Read Acts 16:25-34. Describe the jailer before and after conversion.

Before: _____

After: _____

Evangelism—proclaiming the gospel and making it known—is the heart of a missionary's work. That does not mean that every missionary preaches. But regardless of the assignment, missionaries verbally share their faith in Christ and live His teachings in relationships and holistic ministry. Every means possible that enables us to relate to a lost world, win a credible hearing, and elicit a response can and should be used. That includes education, health care, hunger relief, disaster response, and compassionate pastoral care. Yet it is not what missionaries do but the power of the Holy Spirit that convicts people of sin, convinces them of the truth of the gospel, and draws them to Christ.

Evangelism: *Proclaiming the gospel and making it known*

Although 33 percent of the world's population identify themselves as Christian, most are cultural Christians with no understanding of personal faith in Jesus Christ. Research reveals that about 10 percent of the world's population consists of born-again believers. That is about six hundred million in a global population in excess of six billion. One of 10 is a remarkable number that should make the task of evangelizing the world readily accomplished. However, the problem is one of location. Most of the evangelical Christian population is concentrated in America and a few other evangelized countries, leaving vast population segments around the world with no access to a church or a Christian witness.

Place a mark on the line from *comfortable* to *uncomfortable* to express how you feel about being 1 of 10 who claims a born-again experience.

Comfortable   Uncomfortable

The World in Gospel Perspective

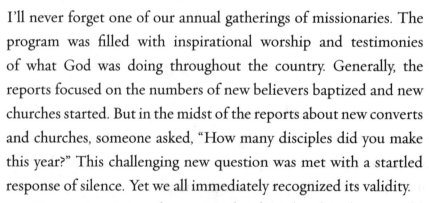

25%   Non-Christians with little or no access to the gospel, **1.56 billion**

42%   Non-Christians with some access to the gospel, **2.64 billion**

23%   Cultural Christianity, **1.4 billion**

10%   Evangelical, Bible-believing Christians, **600 million**
(Baptists, **50 million**)

Missionaries quickly realize they will never be able to reach all the massive population segments in their places of assignment. The result of their witness must be a group of baptized local believers, drawn together by the Holy Spirit into a visible fellowship for worship and witness as a New Testament church. This covenant community becomes a nucleus of witness and ministry, reaching beyond what individual missionaries can do.

I'll never forget one of our annual gatherings of missionaries. The program was filled with inspirational worship and testimonies of what God was doing throughout the country. Generally, the reports focused on the numbers of new believers baptized and new churches started. But in the midst of the reports about new converts and churches, someone asked, "How many disciples did you make this year?" This challenging new question was met with a startled response of silence. Yet we all immediately recognized its validity.

Jesus commissioned us to make disciples, but how would we respond with confidence and credibility? We could count the number of baptisms, but how many of them were truly living for Christ and giving evidence of becoming Christlike followers of the Master in faith and obedience? I began to squirm as I immediately thought of some of the new Christians in my area. They were apparently converts of Jerry Rankin—they had answered all of the right questions—but were struggling in their newfound faith. Their character formation still had a long way to go; I wasn't sure I was ready to identify them as growing disciples of Jesus.

Do you belong to a New Testament church? If so, how would you prove it?

❏ Our pastor preaches mostly from the New Testament.

❏ We try to be like a church in the first century.

❏ Many people join our church each year.

❏ We have great potluck dinners.

❏ Other: _____

I hope you chose *other* and added a more biblical answer! Many see numerical growth as the benchmark. Because the Holy Spirit indwells the church as the body of Christ, it is natural for it to grow numerically through an expanding witness and to multiply by planting new churches. As these local, indigenous churches reproduce and replicate themselves, they become an expanding network that can literally make the gospel accessible to the whole world.

THE END GOAL

The end goal of evangelism is not just to witness to others or even to lead others to accept Christ. Evangelism includes discipling new believers and incorporating them into a local, nurturing fellowship of believers.

> **Discipleship:** *The lifelong journey of obedience to Christ that transforms a person's values and behavior and results in ministry in the home, the church, and the world*

We generally understand discipling as a process of growing in understanding and obedience after the salvation experience. While we rejoice in the millions of people responding to a Christian witness around the world, the IMB does not track or report professions of faith. Whether water baptism immediately follows that decision or comes after an initial period of teaching, it is regarded as the scriptural form of confessing someone's faith. That public step clearly identifies a new believer. It demonstrates that a person has put aside former beliefs and religious adherence to be a follower of Jesus Christ.

We rejoice when people respond to the passing witness of a mission volunteer. Multitudes may indicate their desire to follow Christ in response to a public invitation at a massive crusade. Only God can know the level of understanding and the change that has transpired in someone's heart. But without follow-up, evangelism lacks follow-through. We would be birthing baby Christians and leaving them to fend for themselves. To be discipled, new believers must be incorporated into a church. Converts may have assurance of eternal life, but Christlike learners and followers of Jesus continue to grow in their faith.

What are some ways followers of Jesus grow in their faith?

_____

Kingdom growth occurs only as new believers witness to their neighbors and family, faithfully worship with fellow believers, and minister to the needs around them. Individuals are born again through the message of redemption, but the result is the lordship of Christ. Jesus sent us not just to proclaim the gospel of salvation but also to live the gospel of the kingdom—the reign of Christ in the lives of His people.

IMB Basic Task

Evangelism through proclamation, discipleship, equipping, and ministry
that results in indigenous Baptist churches

Evangelism that leads to new churches is the kind of evangelism that makes disciples. We should preach the gospel to every creature, seek to persuade and win every individual, and make disciples of all nations and peoples. But our mission must never be less than what Jesus told us to do—make disciples.

In the United States church attendance is declining. Check the statements that help explain this downward trend.

❑ Many people don't go to church because they are saved and are guaranteed admittance to heaven, regardless of their worldly actions.

❑ An influx of other religions, sects, and cults has weakened the Christian influence in my community.

❑ Churchgoers have a negative reputation for fights, splits, and hypocrisy.

❑ Sporting events have monopolized Sundays.

❑ Sunday is the only day off in some occupations.

Why is church involvement so essential for discipling new believers?

_____

DAY 5
GOD'S PROVIDENCE AND MISSIONS

If the world is lost and Jesus Christ is our only hope of salvation, then all believers must discover their place in the task God has committed to us. God is using social upheaval, political disruption, economic uncertainty, natural disasters, and wars—so prominent throughout our world today—to stir a search for spiritual answers. As we have moved into the 21st century, God has been working through global events in unprecedented ways to make kingdom growth possible. In fact, to stay abreast of all God is doing has required making fairly radical changes in the way Southern Baptists do missions. That is not to reflect on those who have gone before. Indeed, leadership and strategies in each past generation have been effective. They not only established the kingdom in many countries through a growing network of national churches but also laid the foundation for the current expansion we are seeing.

Following the fall of the Iron Curtain and the disintegration of the Soviet Union, change has been rampant. Global alliances took new forms, opening doors for extending God's kingdom and mission advance. Communication and technology brought the world closer. As we moved into the 21st century, responsiveness to the gospel reached dimensions that were unimaginable a few years earlier. Today ethnic tensions and conflicts are tearing these countries apart. The terrorist actions of September 11, 2001, as many have said, changed our world so that it will never be the same again. Subsequently, eight of our missionaries were martyred, victims of violent deaths within a time span of 26 months. Our sense of security has been shattered, international relations are strained, global economies are in disarray, and warfare against an elusive terrorist enemy appears a likely expectation for years to come.

CHALLENGES LEAD TO CHANGES

There is no question that our world is changing, confronting us with new challenges in fulfilling God's kingdom purpose. Someone has observed that if external changes exceed an organization's internal changes, it is moving toward irrelevance and ineffectiveness. Attitudes shaped by postmodern influences have made an impact on our churches and have challenged traditional denominational programs. We tend to react to the immediate, respond to the urgent, or hold on to the comfort and security of how we have always done things in the past. Only a vision can keep us focused on our kingdom task, put change in perspective, and keep us from being diverted from fulfilling God's purpose.

In central Asia I enjoyed a night of fellowship with pioneer missionaries who had come to this region in response to God's call. They had boldly seized the opportunity to fill challenging assignments in a changing political climate. As we prayed, one of them surprised me by praising God for the 70 years the Soviet Union had dominated the peoples of central Asia. I thought it strange that he would be thankful for that Communist regime.

Later I asked why he prayed as he did. He replied that for centuries the great universities and mosques of central Asia had been strategic in propagating Islam across trade routes and among populous cities. "But," he said, "in a mere 70 years the atheistic influence of the Soviet Union has emasculated this Muslim stronghold, leaving the people empty, spiritually destitute, and responsive to the gospel in this time of harvest."

What is happening in the world today is not a result of IMB strategies and Western diplomacy. God's power is shaking nations. God's providence is behind world events. He has not relinquished His sovereignty over the nations. And when we read of political disruptions, social upheaval, economic deterioration, wars, and natural disasters, He is creating an environment in which people cannot look to their culture, traditions, and religion but only to Jesus for salvation and hope. God has called us, like Esther, into the kingdom for such a time as this!

Providence: *God's care for and guidance of His creation against all opposition*

Review the story of Esther in the Old Testament, especially Esther 4:8-14. What would have been your response to Mordecai? Check all that apply.

❏ Scared   ❏ Courageous
❏ Totally humbled   ❏ Somewhat surprised
❏ Willing   ❏ Bothered and bewildered
❏ Very angry   ❏ No way!

Do you have Mordecai's same sense of urgency from God?
❏ Yes   ❏ No   ❏ Not sure

For years Christians have prayed for those behind the Iron Curtain in Communist countries where religious freedom was prohibited and believers were persecuted. In all of our long-range planning and mission strategies, no one projected the possibility that missionary personnel would freely witness in the former Soviet Union or would once again serve in China. Yet today literally thousands of missionaries and volunteers have swept into those countries. That did not happen as a result of our strategic planning or Western diplomacy but because of the power and providence of God.

FROM CRUMBLING WALLS TO OPEN DOORS

When the walls began to crumble and the doors began to open to the Communist world in the early 1990s, we recognized that one formidable barrier to global evangelization still remained—the Muslim world across northern Africa, the Middle East, and central Asia. However, following the tragic events of September 11, 2001, personnel throughout this region began reporting that people were expressing disillusionment with their Islamic faith. They questioned a religion that would be used to justify terrorist activity. They asked questions that reflected a search for hope and security that only Jesus can provide.

God said through the prophet Haggai, " 'I am going to shake the heavens and the earth. I will overturn royal thrones and destroy the power of the Gentile kingdoms' " (Hag. 2:21-22). This prophecy is being fulfilled as nations are disintegrating and fragmenting in ethnic conflict and as totalitarian powers are being overthrown. God's power is being manifested so that His kingdom might be extended.

> The following is a list of countries being evangelized today. Place a check mark beside those you had never heard of 10 years ago. Can you identify where these are on a world map today? ❏ Yes ❏ No
> ❏ Uzbekistan ❏ Azerbaijan
> ❏ Bosnia-Herzegovina ❏ Bhutan
> ❏ Chechnya ❏ Slovenia
> ❏ Chad ❏ Guinea-Bissau

In 1997 the IMB adopted a strategy called New Directions. It really wasn't new but represented a sharpened focus on what had always been our purpose. The intent was to position us for maximum global impact when we crossed the threshold into the 21st century three years later. Now identified as Strategic Directions for the 21st Century (SD21), these initiatives have resulted in greater advance in global evangelization than anyone could have imagined.

But with growth and increased opportunity came the realization that the task of international missions could not be done by missionaries alone and the limited resources of the IMB. The Great Commission is the responsibility of every local church. We can cooperate to send and support missionaries, but only as every church becomes involved in God's mission can the gospel spread to the ends of the earth. This realization has resulted in a new vision of mobilizing and equipping the local church to reach the nations and peoples of the world. We often speak of God's providence. The word *providence* comes from two Latin words—*video*, which means *to see*, and *pro*, which means *beforehand*. God is able to see beforehand what is going to happen and predetermine how it can be used for His purpose.

Review Jesus' Great Commission in Matthew 28:19-20. List three world events or developments in recent years that are fulfilling Jesus' commission to reach the ends of the earth.

1. _____

2. _____

3. _____

What is your role in fulfilling the Great Commission?
❑ I don't know.
❑ I don't have a role.
❑ I'm doing all I can.
❑ I'm open to a greater role.
❑ I'm excited by the ways God is using me.
❑ Other: _____

_____

_____

1. Name changed for security reasons.
2. H. Ernest Nichol, "We've a Story to Tell," *The Baptist Hymnal* (Nashville: Convention Press, 1991), 586.

WEEK 3
EMPOWERING GOD'S KINGDOM THROUGH PRAYER

VERSE TO REMEMBER

"Confess your sins to one another and pray
for one another, so that you may be healed.
The intense prayer of the righteous is very powerful."

JAMES 5:16

In the words of a Southern Baptist mission volunteer in east Asia: "We had visited an older gentleman to check his vital signs. He had suffered a stroke. We asked if we could pray to our God, the one true God, for his health, and he said yes. On the second day he said his pain was gone and he felt so much better! Just before we left, he told us he would like to know our God! He had never even heard the name of Jesus before meeting us. We prayed a salvation prayer with him, and as I said, "Amen," he said, '*Xie Xie, Jesu. Xie Xie, Jesu. Xie Xie, Jesu!*'—thank You, Jesus!"

In this week's study you will discover how you can become a part of the International Mission Board's strategy for specific missions in specific places. You will be challenged to become a PRAYERPlus Partnership church or to adopt an unreached people group. Do you know why the Lottie Moon Christmas Offering® for International Missions is so vital to our missionaries? Or could you explain why Southern Baptists give to missions through the Cooperative Program? This week your church can begin or continue your missions involvement through prayer and financial support for growing God's kingdom around the world.

DAY 1
GOD'S PROMISE OF POWER

*"You will receive power when the Holy Spirit has come upon you,
and you will be My witnesses in Jerusalem, in all Judea and Samaria,
and to the ends of the earth" (Acts 1:8).*

In 2002 IMB personnel reached 146 previously unreached people groups with the gospel; the following year 131 new people groups heard it for the first time. More than 500,000 baptisms were reported in 2002, and the figure grew to 607,000 the following year. This increase could happen only because of God's power, which indwells the message of the gospel.

A strategy coordinator in China envisioned seeing 200 churches started in his four-year term as he began training national church leaders. But he had to enlarge his vision when more than 200 were started in six months. Three mosques were closed in a city in Africa because so many people became Christian believers. A resistant tribal group in Africa suddenly became responsive, and more than 100,000 have been baptized in the past 10 years. In Algeria seeds of the gospel were planted among Kabyle Berbers, and more than 75 churches now line the valley where they live. Some researchers report that as many as 20,000 new believers are coming to faith in Christ every day in China, and Christians now number somewhere between 75 million and 100 million in spite of government opposition and restrictions.

Reaching almost six billion lost people in our world, including more than four thousand unreached people groups, exceeds the power of human plans and abilities. Our traditional mission methods and our limited resources are inadequate for the challenge. Fulfilling the Great Commission will become a reality only when God empowers our efforts.

CROSS-CULTURAL MISSIONS

Through creative actions missionaries can gain entry to and plant their lives in places that would have been unimaginable just a few years ago. Places restricted to a traditional missionary witness now open doors to Christian teachers, business persons, social workers, computer consultants, health-care personnel, and people serving in many other professions and roles.

The Apostle Paul had a vision and a calling to take the gospel to the Gentiles, the non-Jewish people and nations of his day. Like missionaries today, Paul had to be creative in order to gain entrance to the Gentile world. In Romans 15:18 Paul described his kingdom vision: "I would not dare say anything except what Christ has accomplished through me to make the Gentiles obedient by word and deed."

Rewrite in your own words Romans 15:18 to explain how Paul approached his God-given task.

_____

Paul is a prototype of a cross-cultural missionary. He testified to this calling throughout his epistles and the Book of Acts. In Romans 15 he affirmed that the only thing worthy of boasting or speaking about is what we have allowed Christ to do through us to bring the nations to faith in the one true God. That is God's purpose.

As God's witness, what do you pray for? Underline your answer(s).
- Opportunities to share the gospel
- The words to say
- Courage
- Empowerment
- Sensitivity to the unsaved
- I don't pray about witnessing.

Paul observed in Romans 15:19 that God's redemptive purpose was accomplished "by the power of miraculous signs and wonders, and by the power of God's Spirit." It was not what Paul himself had done; God's power enabled him to proclaim the gospel and plant churches all the way from Jerusalem to Illyricum. In Scripture God assures us of only one absolute use of His power. We will be His witnesses both in " 'Jerusalem, in all Judea and Samaria, and to the ends of the earth' " (Acts 1:8). We can pray for God's blessing on our church programs, and He will bless them if they are in accord with His will and for His glory. But He has given us the power of the Holy Spirit to go beyond the walls of our churches to witness to a lost world.

We must never forget that the Great Commission in Matthew 28:19-20 is preceded by Christ's claim in verse 18 that " 'all authority [power] has been given to Me in heaven and on earth.' " Because of His power and authority, Christ promises to go with us—even to the most remote village—in confidence that we will disciple the nations.

IMB Basic Commitment
Obedience to the lordship of Christ and God's infallible Word

FOUNDATIONAL PRINCIPLES
Obedience to the lordship of Christ and obedience to the Bible as our sole authority of faith and practice are foundational principles for our Baptist beliefs and mission. We make plans and begin programs that are quite diverse. Goals can take us in any number of directions.

But all we do must be superseded by a higher commitment to Jesus Christ—the eternal, incarnate, living Son of God—and to God's inspired, authoritative Word.

> We speak of Jesus as being the incarnation of God. What does it mean to send missionary personnel to be incarnational witnesses?

_____

Jesus is our Savior and Lord; obedience to His commands and commitment to follow His revealed will are not optional. The power Jesus claimed in Matthew 28:18 has been made available to us to disciple the nations and to extend God's kingdom to the ends of the earth. All that remain are our obedience and commitment.

> Explain why a commitment to these foundational principles is essential to receiving God's power to win the lost.

The lordship of Jesus Christ: _____

_____

God's infallible Word: _____

_____

DAY 2
THE INVOLVEMENT OF GOD'S PEOPLE

No one gets an exemption from the teaching and mandate of Scripture to reach a lost world. Churches and volunteer groups can participate in unlimited ministries when they have a heart for the world, give their lives in obedience to God's call, and trust the power of God's Spirit to use them as His witnesses. This purpose reveals God's heart for lost people groups, as well as for lost individuals. Scripture does not limit our realm of responsibility to where we live, and if we don't take the gospel to the lost—wherever they are—who will?

Read Genesis 12:2-3. Why did God promise to bless Abraham?

_____

OUR MOST VALUABLE RESOURCE

Most churches have never had a missionary called out of their congregations. Could that reflect the fact that the church does not demonstrate a heart for the world—that it isn't burdened and praying for the nations? We considered it "bold mission thrust" when Southern Baptists finally had more than five thousand overseas missionaries. But that represents a minuscule number relative to the needs of a lost world. In fact, it is only one missionary unit for every 1.6 million people. But those five thousand missionaries represent only .03 percent of Southern Baptist members—fewer than one for every three thousand. Why don't more people hear God's call? Why do so few have a heart for the lost, most of whom have no opportunity to hear of Jesus?

I cannot wipe from my mind an illustration I once read. The picture is that final judgment day when we will don our white robes of righteousness and be welcomed into the eternal glory of heaven. We will celebrate and rejoice as we give glory to the Lamb of God, who redeemed us from sin. But across a great chasm will be a multitude of people with bowed heads and sad faces entering an eternity of torment in hell—those who never heard or responded to the message of salvation. They will look at us with forlorn reconciliation to their fate, and that look will say, "You knew, but you never came and told us! We never had an opportunity to know."

But sadder still will be the eyes of our Lord. In one of those paradoxes of the Christian faith, even as He receives us with joy, His heart will be broken over the multitudes who never knew that He died for them. I believe His eyes will meet ours much as they did Peter's on that night of denial and without a word will communicate, "I told you to go. I promised you My power. I assured you of My grace, but you were unwilling to go so that My kingdom could be extended to the ends of the earth."

We often say that our most valuable resource is the personnel who plant their lives and build friendships among people who are lost. The lost often reject our words and are closed to our Christian worldview, but a flesh-and-blood witness reflecting the difference Christ makes effectively convinces people of the truth of the gospel. Is this not why Jesus left heaven to come to a sinful world?

We can do many things to evangelize the world. Certainly, distributing Bibles and Christian literature are invaluable methods. We effectively use media more than ever through radio, film, CD, DVD, and the Internet. Although all of these present an impersonal witness, God uses them to touch the hearts of those who are open and searching for spiritual truth. However, those who respond need friends who can reply to questions, clarify confused perceptions, and then disciple and train new believers. The IMB exists for the purpose of sending and supporting missionary personnel who do just that.

Incarnational witness: *Living in flesh and blood a testimony of our faith so that our behavior and lifestyle are a witness to the people around us. Allowing people to see Jesus in us gives credibility to a verbal witness.*

Who has been an incarnational witness in your life? How did their influence make a difference in your openness to follow Jesus' commands?

_____

_____

IMB Basic Strategy

Send and support gifted, God-called missionaries who, with mutual respect, accountability, and cooperation, carry out the Great Commission in an incarnational witness

HEARING GOD'S CALL

A man in Texas had retired early from the ministry because of his health. Since retirement he had started a prayer ministry and spent several hours a day in prayer. He wrote me to say that he regularly prayed for the IMB and for me. He consistently received materials from our prayer office and systematically prayed for the missionaries listed and for their needs.

His letter described his great burden about the need for more missionary personnel. He had heard stories of the people groups who had no one to share the gospel with them. He explained that whenever he prayed, he always linked his prayers with a Scripture, and he had been praying Matthew 9:38: " 'Pray to the Lord of the harvest to send out workers into His harvest.' " He concluded by asking, "Dr. Rankin, why isn't God answering my prayer? Why isn't He calling out the laborers who are needed around the world?"

I wasn't sure how to answer him. I had been wondering the same thing myself. Later I read an article that provided an answer. It quoted a 19th-century missions advocate who observed, "God is calling out the laborers ... but the laborers are not responding because of a closed mind, a calloused heart, or a reluctant will!"

> Check reasons you think people are not open to hearing God's call.
> ❑ We have enough missionaries.
> ❑ We need to concentrate on winning the lost where we live before we go to other places.
> ❑ God has chosen not to call many who would be willing to go.
> ❑ We can fulfill God's call by supporting those who go and letting them do missions on our behalf.
> ❑ People who are afraid of the dangers overseas are unwilling to risk their security and comfortable lifestyles.
> ❑ People lack concern for the lost in other lands.
> ❑ People lack awareness of the needs and opportunities.
> ❑ Our words and actions don't indicate that Christ is our Lord and Master.

I hope you checked all of these reasons we give for withholding our commitment to God's will for reaching the lost. Why does God tell us to pray for Him to send out laborers? Isn't God the one who calls? Isn't He capable of stirring their hearts without our help? Yes, but just maybe you are the one He wants to hear that call. And just maybe He wants to use your church to help get the job done. When we pray for a lost world and our hearts become burdened for the peoples and nations in darkness, our closed minds become open to the possibilities of how God can use us to bring His light to the darkness. When we pray, our calloused, self-centered hearts are softened and broken for those who have no opportunity to know Jesus. Our reluctant wills become submissive, and we are willing to say, "Here I am. Send me" (Isa. 6:8).

DAY 3
THE POTENTIAL OF PRAYER

Early in my tenure as the president of the IMB, I mentioned in a missions message that the IMB had recently appointed our first missionary unit to serve openly in Albania. After the service a woman approached me. Crying and overcome with emotion, she asked, "Do we really have a missionary in Albania?" I assured her that we did. She explained that seven years earlier she had read that Albania was the most atheistic country in the world, prohibiting worship and all religious expression. She had called the Foreign Mission Board, as we were known then, to ask what we were doing in Albania. She was told that the country was closed to a missionary presence; we could do nothing but pray.

"I asked our ladies' group at church to pray for Albania," she said. "For seven years we have been praying for Albania!" When I heard that testimony, I began to weep also. No doubt the doors to Albania opened to the gospel because a small group of women had a heart for a lost nation and interceded in prayer before God's throne. Certainly, other circumstances brought about the change, such as the collapse of Communism in eastern Europe. But those who have seen global changes open doors that had long been closed to the gospel readily acknowledge that God, in His sovereign power over nations, moves in response to the prayers of His people. Strongholds crumble and the response to the gospel accelerates when we pray.

PRAYER FOR THE NATIONS

God gives us an amazing promise in Psalm 2:8:

> *"Ask of Me,*
> *and I will make the nations Your inheritance*
> *and the ends of the earth Your possession."*

In this verse what does God promise to do if we pray for the nations?

_____

How often do we pray for Sudan, Libya, Afghanistan, Eritrea, Bhutan, and Chad? Do we fervently plead for unreached people groups such as the Drukpa, the Mazaderani, the Acehnese, and the Baluchi? Is it any wonder that generation after generation in these places continues in the bondage of darkness and sin when God yearns to draw them into His kingdom?

Name countries and people groups that you regularly pray for.

_____

Most of our prayers are about ourselves, our personal needs and concerns, our families, our communities, and our churches. Does it seldom occur to us to intercede for the nations? Satan's strongholds remain secure against the kingdom of God when we fail to pray. Why would God, who is sovereign over the nations, limit what He does to the prayers of His people? Scripture reveals a God who calls us to prayer so that we can know His heart and can have the privilege of participating in what He is doing.

Missionaries faithfully labor and struggle in resistant fields. They fight discouragement and persevere in the face of religious opposition, government restrictions, illness, and conflict. Meanwhile, churches and faithful givers often voice their GBM prayers (God bless the missionaries) with a shallow concern that doesn't bother to lift specific needs of specific missionaries and plead for the people they seek to reach.

How can you find specific prayer requests for missionaries and their work?

_____

For information about prayer needs, go to _www.imb.org_. This Web site provides much information about the IMB and ways you can encourage missionaries. A big part of the IMB's strategy is coordinated prayer by thousands of intercessors.

So why does God call us to pray for the nations? Because when we pray for the peoples whom God seeks to draw into His kingdom, we begin to share His burden and become responsive to what He wants us to do. Without prayer, as an individual or a church, we are left to our own devices, wisdom, and insights. We struggle to make things happen and strive to make our programs successful. Prayer is not meant to undergird and support the mission strategies we as an organization plan. In prayer God reveals Himself and His plans and stirs His people's hearts to join Him where He is working. The act of praying opens our hearts to hear God's voice about the work He wants to do.

Does God know how the people of the world will be reached? Of course! Does He know the churches and people who will be called to be His instruments to reach each specific people group? Yes. He knows the one who will respond as the result of a missionary's testimony, a mission trip, or a news event. He knows those who, with obedient hearts, will begin to pray. When those prayers begin, God moves in hearts, directing His people to carry out His plan.

Read the account of Paul and Barnabas's call as missionaries in Acts 13:2. What was the church doing?

_____

Who took the initiative in setting apart Paul and Barnabas?

_____

Paul and Barnabas did not walk the aisle at invitation time to surrender to full-time service, telling the church that God had called them to go as missionaries. No, the church was fasting and praying, and God revealed that it was to send out Paul and Barnabas for the work to which God had called them. If churches would begin to pray for the nations and unreached people groups, God would likely call out the missionaries He needs for the task from within those congregations.

GOD'S RESPONSE WHEN WE PRAY

Approximately what proportion of your daily prayer time is spent on the following topics? List percentages that total 100 percent.

Praising and thanking God: _____

Confessing known sin: _____

Personal needs: _____

Your immediate family and their needs: _____

Friends and relatives: _____

Unsaved acquaintances: _____

Your church programs and staff: _____

Our country and its leaders: _____

Missionaries and their work: _____

Specific unreached nations and people groups: _____

We are told to pray to the Lord of the harvest so that we might become the answer to those prayers. We don't pray in order to get God to do what we want done. Instead, we enter a relationship with God and talk with Him until we begin to feel His heartbeat As a result, we bring our lives into conformity with what He is already doing and with what He desires to be done.

DAY 4

PRAYER AS MISSION STRATEGY

If you were a missionary, what needs would you tell others to pray about for you? List some requests.

_____

Ask any missionary, "What is your greatest need?" and the reply will always be "Prayer!" They could easily say their greatest need is a more comfortable home, better sanitation, social outlets for their family, or a more secure environment. They could mention better relationships with national co-workers and their mission team or a spiritual breakthrough and a harvest to emerge among their people group. Regardless of their field of assignment, missionary personnel could enumerate needs such as additional missionary reinforcements and more ministry funds for their programs of work. Most of them live in challenging cross-cultural situations that require an austere lifestyle. But they realize that God is the source and provision for every need.

The heart of our strategy to reach the nations and fulfill the Great Commission is prayer. When God's people unite our hearts in prayer, we are acknowledging a need for something we cannot provide ourselves. When we intercede in agreement for the multiplicity of needs on the mission field, our prayers transcend the distance, flow through God's heart, open the portals of His grace, and connect with the missionary in real time.

The battle for the nations will be won on the knees of God's people;
we send the missionaries in for the mopping-up exercises!

NEW CHALLENGES TO PRAYER FOR MISSIONARIES

For many years Southern Baptists have faithfully followed various versions of a prayer calendar, listing missionaries according to their birthdays. Though they may not know the missionaries or their particular needs, they lift these names to the Father in intercession. Those who pray have confidence that God, who knows their needs, will bless the missionaries in a special way. Missionaries often testify that when thousands of people intercede on their behalf, a breakthrough occurs, whether in their outreach efforts, an unusual response to their witness, or a family or personal need being met.

On missionary Lynn Nelson's birthday, she and her family traveled with 14 nationals from Buwama to the Butebi village to meet with the Baganda team's Bible-study groups from Mityana, Mubende, and other Ugandan villages. Lynn received her first birthday gift when she learned that more than three hundred unsaved people were present. Her next present was seeing a nonbeliever from their Buwama group express his heart to God in a solo song. But the highlight of Lynn's birthday was seeing her middle daughter baptized. Her daughter said, "The people in America know about Jesus and have many churches to tell about Him. The Ugandans do not have that, and I want to be an example of Jesus and show them that no one should fear water." The prayers of God's people made a life-changing difference in the lives of Lynn's family and in the lives of those they work to reach for Christ.

Ministering among the Mestizos of Querétaro, Mexico, missionary Jody Fleming shares, "We praise the Lord for the power of prayer! My birthday prayer was for the family of A. and L. to know the Lord as their personal Savior. They stopped by one night when a friend from Oklahoma was visiting us. The discussion quickly turned to topics of the Bible. A. said that he had many questions, and we continued to answer each one as it led closer and closer to the question we wanted to hear. When he asked us, 'You mean all my good works won't get me to heaven?' we knew the Holy Spirit had prepared his heart. After we showed him and his wife what the Bible says, he turned to his wife and said, 'I want to invite Jesus into my heart, don't you?' With tears she said, 'Yes,' and another prayer was answered. Praise the Lord!"

We are grateful that so many Southern Baptists are conscientious about faithfully praying for missionaries on their birthdays each year. But an increasing number of personnel cannot be listed on a prayer calendar identifying them as missionaries. They serve in restricted countries through legitimate roles that allow them access to the people and provide a witness where it would not otherwise be possible. If their names appeared on a published list or on the Internet identifying them as missionaries, they would likely lose their platform—their basis for being in the country—and be deported. Worse still, revealing their identities could jeopardize their safety and the lives of local believers.

Currently, more than 40 percent of the personnel serving overseas with the IMB are in places where they cannot be identified as missionaries. As a generic identification these places are called the Last Frontier because they literally represent the last frontier of completing the Great Commission. Sometimes these missionaries are listed only by their initials or first names without a specific location being identified.

Traditional prayer intercessors, accustomed to knowing for whom they are praying and where they serve, may become frustrated. But God knows exactly who those initials represent, where they are, and what their needs are that day. He knows missionaries serving in the Last Frontier who have birthdays that may not be listed on the prayer calendar at all, and He will hear and answer the prayers of faithful prayer warriors who intercede without even knowing for whom they are praying.

Do you know a missionary by name?   ❑ Yes   ❑ No
Do you pray for missionaries on their birthdays?   ❑ Yes   ❑ No

What it would take for you to pray for a specific missionary
in a specific country?
❑ A miracle
❑ More concern than I have felt before
❑ Information from the IMB
❑ A call by God
❑ Other: _____
_____

A PRAYERPLUS PARTNERSHIP

Every missionary should have a base of prayer support. Personal relationships enable missionaries in Last Frontier assignments to share where they are serving and communicate sensitive needs that could never be published. The churches who pray for them by name understand the security precautions and can handle prayer requests discreetly. Many churches have adopted multiple missionary families, sometimes leading every Sunday School department or class to adopt a family, communicate with them, encourage them, and intercede on their behalf.

Just as it would be unthinkable to send missionaries to the field and not assure them of financial support, it would be irresponsible to allow them to go overseas into Satan's territory without the assurance of critical prayer support. When a church commits to pray for an adopted people group, country, or population segment, it enters a PRAYERPlus Partnership. A PRAYERPlus Partnership church makes a commitment to partner with the IMB by praying for an unreached people group. Prayer is something everyone can do. It doesn't cost a thing, nor does it necessarily infringe on an already overcommitted church budget.

However, there is a contingency—the plus. The church commits to do whatever God leads it to do. Such a prayer commitment may mean providing research or developing a communication network among various mission groups seeking to reach that particular people. It may mean sending volunteer teams, responding to special needs of a missionary family, or providing resources for the *Jesus* film or other tools for outreach and discipleship.

PRAYERPlus: *A partnership that links a church with an unengaged people group identified by overseas field leadership*

***Jesus* film:** *A two-hour docudrama about the life of Christ, based on the Gospel of Luke. The film, distributed by Campus Crusade for Christ, has been seen in every country of the world and has been translated into hundreds of languages since its initial release in 1979.*

Could your church become part of a PRAYERPlus Partnership?
Explain why or why not.

_____

_____

SPIRITUAL WARFARE

Can you imagine one day finding around God's throne a group of Beja from the Sudan or Wolof from Senegal included in that gathering because you and your church prayed them into the kingdom? We need to realize that to pray for peoples in darkness means engaging in warfare against powers and principalities. Scripture makes it clear that spiritual warfare is inevitable. Missionaries are literally venturing into Satan's territory—the peoples, countries, and cultures that do not know Jesus Christ and are literally Satan's dominion. The people who dwell in these lands are in bondage to principalities and to the prince of the air. They do not know about anything other than the fears and superstitions with which they have lived all their lives. As one new believer in a Last Frontier country said after hearing and responding to the gospel, "When you are born in the darkness and live your life in the darkness, you never know there is light." The eyes of the lost are blind to the truth of the gospel.

Missionaries and intercessors must be sure they have put on their spiritual armor and are personally equipped for the battle. But Ephesians 6:18 adds, "With every prayer and request, pray at all times in the Spirit, and stay alert in this, with all perseverance and intercession for all the saints."

Check the items that represent your commitment to pray for missionaries.
❑ I will regularly pray for the specific needs of a missionary family.
❑ I will ask God to place an unreached people group or city on my heart, and I will intercede for it faithfully.
❑ I will pray for my church's role in reaching the ends of the earth.
❑ I will make a commitment in my prayers to be open to whatever role God wants me to have personally in reaching the ends of the earth.

KINGDOM PRAYING

So how do we claim the nations and peoples of the world for Christ and enable them to become a part of His kingdom? James 4:2 tells us that "you do not have because you do not ask." Scripture promises amazing answers to prayer when we ask in accordance with the Father's will and when we make our requests consistent with that which will glorify Him. We have already seen that God's heart and desire are to be exalted among the nations, but how much do we pray for His name to be lifted up among all peoples of the earth?

A few churches and individuals have ventured into true kingdom praying, beseeching God for the nations and peoples of the world. Your church may not be able to pray systematically for all 11,249 people groups around the world, but if your church adopted a specific people group and church members poured out their hearts on its behalf, the barriers would vanish, doors would open, Satan's strongholds would crumble, and the power of the gospel would begin to bring people into God's kingdom.

Acts 4:31 records about the early church, "When they had prayed, ... they were all filled with the Holy Spirit and began to speak God's message with boldness." Prayer enables us to participate in the providential work of God's Spirit as He moves among the nations, claiming them for His possession.

Rather than just praying that God would bless the missionaries, list specific needs for which you could pray. Compare your list with other members' ideas at your next group session.

_____

_____

_____

_____

DAY 5
GIVING: BLESSED TO BE A BLESSING

Missionaries alone could not extend God's kingdom to the ends of the earth without the cooperative support and involvement of God's people. The exciting advance of God's kingdom thrives in part because Southern Baptists discovered channels for personal involvement in the task. With more than just a responsibility to support the work of missionaries, churches are responding to an increasing number of short-term volunteer opportunities. Other churches are needed to come alongside overseas missionaries in partnerships that reinforce their strategies, supplement their efforts, and multiply their witness.

HISTORIC COOPERATION

The Southern Baptist Convention was founded in 1845 to consolidate the efforts of many independent, regional mission societies then in existence. It sought to create cooperation through a unified Domestic Mission Board and Foreign Mission Board. W. B. Johnson, one of the founding leaders of the Southern Baptist Convention, urged the churches to send messengers to the initial organizational convention in Augusta, Georgia, and challenged these independent societies to convene "for the purpose of organizing a practical plan on which the energies of the whole Baptist denomination may be elicited, combined and directed in one sacred effort for sending the word of life to idolatrous lands."[1]

Even then our visionary founders realized that churches could do more together than they could separately through isolated, fragmented efforts. Because Baptists believe in and practice the priesthood of believers and the autonomy of each local church, only voluntary cooperation links our churches together as a denomination. While we share common doctrines and beliefs, much diversity exists in styles of worship and local ministries. No ecclesiastical authority compels us to work together to fulfill the Great Commission. Our churches do so because they have a common commitment to the lordship of Jesus Christ.

Years ago Southern Baptists abandoned a societal approach in which each institution and ministry competed for direct funding and support. The Cooperative Program was established to enable each church to voluntarily allocate a percentage of its undesignated receipts to the work of the denomination. Today those combined gifts provide the basic resources to support the local state conventions, six seminaries, other denominational ministries and services, and mission efforts throughout North America and around the world.

The annual Lottie Moon Christmas Offering® for International Missions allows churches to combine additional resources to send and support missionaries so that they do not have to personally raise their support before fulfilling their callings. Since the founding of the Southern Baptist Convention, more than 18,000 missionaries have been sent around the globe to extend God's kingdom, assured that Southern Baptist churches would provide their support.

Cooperative Program: *A partnership of missions support launched in 1925 among individual Southern Baptists, churches, state conventions, and Southern Baptist Convention entities. Southern Baptists support missions in their state, nation, and world by giving through the Cooperative Program.*

Lottie Moon Christmas Offering for International Missions: *An annual offering collected by Southern Baptist churches for the sole purpose of supporting international missions. The offering is named for Charlotte Diggs Moon, a missionary to China for 39 years, who first suggested that Southern Baptists collect money at Christmastime to support foreign missions.*

What amount did your church give to missions through the Lottie Moon Christmas Offering for International Missions last year? _____
How much was that per member? _____
What percentage of the annual budget does your church designate to God's work through the Cooperative Program? _____ percent

A BETTER WAY

The average Southern Baptist church has fewer than three hundred resident members. Many churches, even those that are much larger, struggle to support their staffs and respond to the challenges of local ministries. Few would be able on their own to send and support missionaries to proclaim the gospel to foreign lands and to our own country's pioneer areas. But through cooperation more than 10,000 God-called missionaries are able to serve through the North American and International Mission Boards today.

In addition to baptizing new believers and starting new churches around the world, in 2005 international missionaries reported involvement in training 21,899 pastors, church leaders, and students in residential seminaries and Bible schools. Another 128,010 participated in programs of extension training on the mission field. Books and tracts were published in multiple languages. Millions heard the good news of salvation through television, films, and radio broadcasts. Multitudes received aid and ministry in the aftermath of floods, droughts, earthquakes, and other disasters. Millions received treatment in mission hospitals and clinics.

I recently read a report from a well-known mission agency indicating that it had had more than 700 applicants for missionary service the previous year. Of that number 240 had been approved and completed training, but eventually, only 74 reached the field. The rest were unable to raise sufficient support. Another organization reported a 30 percent attrition rate because its missionaries could not sustain their support after reaching the field. Some criticized Southern Baptists' system of guaranteed support, claiming that it was not faith-based. But it takes a great deal of faith to send out more than five thousand missionaries and then trust God to move in Southern Baptists' hearts to give an annual offering of more than one hundred million dollars and support a yearly budget of more than a quarter billion dollars!

Why do you think God has blessed and prospered America?
Southern Baptists? you personally?

_____

_____

ACCOUNTABILITY FOR RESOURCES

Each year Southern Baptists increase their gifts to the Cooperative Program and annual mission offerings. Yet the increases are minuscule relative to the challenge of what is needed to reach a lost world. In 2003 missionary appointments were deferred for the first time since the years of the Great Depression because the number of candidates responding to God's call exceeded the resources being provided by the churches. In each of the two previous years more than one thousand new missionaries were approved and sent to the field. The numbers of those being called are not coincidental. God is opening more doors of witness than ever before and is accelerating a global harvest.

How will we give account to the Lord of the harvest for retaining more and more of our financial resources for our local ministries while ignoring the responsibility to reach the ends of the earth? Not long ago the average Southern Baptist church gave more than 10 percent of its undesignated offerings to the Cooperative Program. Commendably, some churches continue to give as much as 20 percent and 30 percent beyond their local church budgets. However, the average allocation has now dropped below 7 percent. That means that churches retain 93 percent of budget receipts for their own needs.

Of the portion that is passed on to the work of the denomination, an average of 64 percent is used by the state convention. Of the remaining 36 percent channeled to the Southern Baptist Convention (of the 7 percent churches allocate to the Cooperative Program), half is designated to the IMB. That calculates to a little more than 1 percent of the undesignated receipts of 43,000 churches that is given to reach the world beyond our borders.

Why do you think the percentage churches give to international missions has declined during the past few years?

_____

Does your church have a plan to increase its giving in coming years?
❑ Yes   ❑ No

When all receipts are taken into consideration, including mission offerings, building funds, and other special gifts, Southern Baptist churches reported receiving 9.6 billion dollars in their offering plates in 2004 alone. Of that amount less than 2.5 percent was channeled to the IMB to evangelize six billion lost people around the world.

A lack of resources is not a problem of the economy; God has prospered and blessed Southern Baptists. He calls us to cooperate to provide missionary support and underwrite the ministries that will take the gospel to all peoples. The Cooperative Program is not an end in itself. It is the means through which every church can have a part in kingdom growth in its state, throughout North America, and to the ends of the earth. The challenge is to bring our hearts into conformity with God's purpose and priorities and to share His passion for reaching our world with the good news of Jesus.

Check ways you are willing to give to your church's budget to provide resources for God's purposes to the ends of the earth.

❑ Tithe
❑ Offerings over the tithe
❑ Mission offerings, such as Lottie Moon
❑ Disaster relief
❑ World hunger and relief ministries
❑ Mission trips
❑ Other: _____

_____

Southern Baptist missionary Lottie Moon is an example of one servant who gave her all. In 1912, during a time of war and famine, Moon silently starved, knowing that her beloved Chinese didn't have enough food. On Christmas Eve she went to be with her Lord, but her legacy lives on. Her model of sacrificial giving is a challenge to us all.

"How many there are ... who imagine that because Jesus paid it all,
they need pay nothing, forgetting that the prime object
of their salvation was that they should follow in the footsteps
of Jesus Christ in bringing back a lost world to God."
—LOTTIE MOON; TUNGCHOW, CHINA; SEPTEMBER 15, 1887

1. W. B. Johnson, in William R. Estep, *Whole Gospel, Whole World* (Nashville: Broadman & Holman Publishers, 1994), 61.

WEEK 4
ENGAGING THE WHOLE WORLD

VERSE TO REMEMBER

" 'God loved the world in this way: He gave His One
and Only Son, so that everyone who believes in Him
will not perish but have eternal life.' "

JOHN 3:16

God has moved so dramatically among one Last Frontier people
group in south Asia that missionaries are shifting their focus to
another unreached people group. One missionary said, "People
discouraged us, saying the people were hard-hearted, that the work
would be fruitless. Today we're looking at about three thousand
believers—most of them people who have come to faith in the past
two years."[1]

Until about 20 years ago missionary efforts were limited to countries that welcomed a
missionary presence. More than 1/3 of the world remained untouched. In 1997 the International Mission Board gave priority to deploying personnel and initiating strategies among all
unreached people groups with populations of one million people or more. Creative strategies
were developed from a conscientious sense of responsibility to take the gospel to all peoples.
Government restrictions continue to keep some peoples unreached. Religious opposition and
cultural traditions often create resistance to the gospel, and these barriers must be overcome.
This week discover how the IMB places missionaries in strategic assignments. God is at work
in our day to fulfill His mission, and He is calling us to finish the task.

DAY 1
EMPLOYING A FOCUSED STRATEGY

The reason any missionary goes overseas, regardless of role or assignment, is a passion to tell a lost world about Jesus. A strategy for proclaiming the gospel and evangelizing the lost must go beyond winning as many individuals as possible. Evangelism must result in local, indigenous churches that become a nucleus of ongoing witness beyond what one missionary can do. We now realize that the only way everyone can ultimately hear and respond to the gospel is if these churches reproduce themselves. We call this strategy church-planting movements. In the activity below, see if you can identify why this strategy works.

Why is it important for evangelism to result in churches? _____

_____

THE IMPORTANCE OF STRATEGIC PLANNING

Strategy is a military term that means *a plan or technique for accomplishing a goal.* It implies that something stands in the way of reaching the desired objective. In the task of claiming the peoples of the world for Jesus Christ, strategy definitely entails spiritual warfare against the principalities and powers of darkness. The task of missions demands wisdom and discernment. We at the IMB would be irresponsible if we approached this awesome task in a passive or haphazard way. We must not accept simply doing what we can and being satisfied with whatever may result.

Strategy: *A plan or technique for accomplishing a goal*

Why should missionaries and church partners have a strategy
for what they do?

_____

The urgency of the moment can easily take our vision off the overall objective. A strategic focus keeps us from simply doing more of what we have already been doing in other places without results. Our focus keeps us from depleting resources on secondary ministries and projects that do not lead to our main objective of kingdom growth. An intentional strategy keeps us from isolating any one aspect of our task to the neglect of others.

Underline which action will result in reaching more people with the gospel.
• Strengthening one local church by adding converts over a period of time
• Multiplying believers by sharing Christ among a whole people group

We at the IMB know where we want to go. We want to plant churches that make the gospel accessible to all peoples, so we must not take roads that lead elsewhere. If we are diverted by the urgency of the moment, we can easily take our vision off the overall objective. Focus is lost when anyone assumes that the physical presence of a short- or long-term missionary, plus well-meaning ministries, becomes the end rather than a means to an end.

STRATEGY LEADS TO PLANTING CHURCHES

Indigenous church-planting movements provide the only way the gospel will be made accessible to all peoples. That's why the IMB does not have a common global strategy. The world is too diverse for a common approach. Cultures and languages are different. Responsiveness varies. The history and maturity of Baptist partners differ all over the world. Fortunately, we have a focused purpose and a unified vision to bring all peoples to saving faith in Jesus Christ.

Church-planting movement: *A rapidly multiplying increase of indigenous churches planting churches among a people group or population segment*

If you could assign only one new missionary unit (person or family), which option would you choose for deployment in each pair of alternatives below? Be prepared to explain why.

❑ Where people are responding to the gospel
❑ Where people have not yet had an opportunity to hear the gospel

❑ Where several other missionary units are working
❑ Where there are no other missionary units

❑ Where churches have already been established
❑ Where there are no churches to be a witness among the people

Does an emphasis on indigenous church-planting movements imply that other kinds of mission work—such as health care, agriculture, social work, and theological education—are not important? Does promoting an awareness of the many still unreached people groups imply that reaping the harvest on open, evangelized fields is not a valid need? Does changing organizational structures and field strategies to be more relevant for the future mean that previous methodologies were ineffective? Not at all!

Focus is not a matter of either/or but one of choosing priorities. An unwillingness to focus on strategic priorities contributes to mediocrity. A budget dollar can be spent only once. Personnel can be deployed only in one place or another. We must make choices if the objective of fulfilling the Great Commission is to be accomplished. We don't choose between good and bad or effective or ineffective; that would be easy. Determining priorities requires a resolve and commitment to what most effectively fulfills our purpose.

> If everyone in the world is to have an opportunity to hear and respond
> to the gospel, check the method that has proved to be most effective.
> ❏ 1. Missionaries witnessing to as many people as they possibly can
> ❏ 2. Baptizing as many people as possible among those responsive
>   to the gospel
> ❏ 3. Discipling new believers and starting churches in every people group
> ❏ 4. Widespread proclamation of the gospel through media

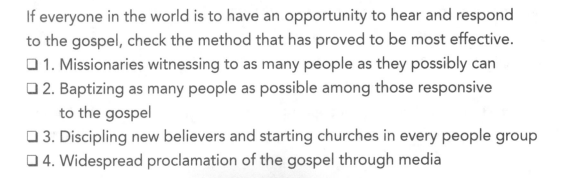

DAY 2
UTILIZING COMPREHENSIVE METHODS

Church-planting movements are accelerating the harvest and providing access to the gospel beyond our missionary witness. Throughout the world the amazing synergy of missionaries working with local Baptists and networking with other evangelicals allows God's power to work in a fruitful way. What happened in the region of south Asia illustrates this truth.

GAINING ENTRY TO RESTRICTED COUNTRIES

For years Southern Baptist missionaries tried to gain entry into India. Entry was not derailed by government restrictions or religious opposition. The India Christian Council, to whom the government relinquished oversight of Christian missionaries, simply would not grant permission. But due to the expertise and credentials of Dr. Jasper McPhail, a cardiovascular surgeon, the opportunity for a medical ministry emerged. Once the door was opened, the ministries and impact of Southern Baptists continued to expand.

God-called physicians joined the team, along with nurses and a lab technician. Nutritionists and community health workers initiated programs that reached into far-flung villages and touched an impoverished society at its point of need. Agricultural consultants, university teachers, and student workers expanded the witness. Business consultants brought in knowledge and technical assistance that increased self-sufficiency and improved the quality of life. All of these, in their distinct and unique ways, cultivated hearts to receive the Christian message.

Why do you think this diverse group of gifted personnel left their comfort zones in America to go to India?

_____

These missionaries were motivated by compassion for the people of India and a recognition that their experience and training had equipped them for a unique contribution. While carrying out their assignments with integrity, they gave encouragement and training to the multiplying house churches that were springing up around them.

So it is all over the world. This historical pattern in India is being replicated in countries long restricted to a missionary presence. People with comprehensive skills and professional experience are accepting assignments that open doors of opportunity to share the gospel.

DIVERSITY IS KEY

In addition to appointing and sending out evangelists and church planters, scores of personnel requests call for a diversity of vocational skills to fill critical niches in mission strategies. In fact, more than one hundred categories of missionary assignment exist. These include accountants and business managers to handle the support needed by more than five thousand personnel involved in 184 countries around the world.

There are requests for the full spectrum of health-care workers, including doctors with various specialties, nurses, public-health workers, and medical technicians. As people with these skills continue to flow to the field, they are no longer restricted to an institutional mission hospital but are teaching in government medical schools and extending a healing ministry in remote locations that have no Christian witness. Today agriculturists, veterinarians, development workers, media specialists, sports trainers, computer technicians, English teachers—people with almost every conceivable skill—have a place on the mission field. Many of these are providing a platform for access into restricted countries that do not allow a missionary presence.

Check each professional or vocational skill that God could use on the mission field.

❑ Coach ❑ Engineer ❑ Computer technician ❑ Accountant
❑ Nutritionist ❑ Business/sales ❑ Attorney ❑ Farmer
❑ Construction ❑ Teacher ❑ Mechanic ❑ Nurse
Others: _____

If individuals who have never heard the gospel are to come to faith in Jesus Christ, someone has to take the gospel to them. While preachers, evangelists, and church planters represent the cutting edge of witness, fewer than 30 percent of IMB personnel are assigned to those categories of service. For the task to be accomplished, skilled personnel engaged in media, publications, medical ministries, and scores of other platforms must open doors, touch hearts, and create an environment for response. However, every missionary must be involved in evangelism, discipleship, training, and church planting to ensure the desired results.

MAKING STRATEGIC DECISONS

The IMB will always struggle with the tension between dispersion or concentration of missionary personnel. With limited numbers of missionaries, what is an appropriate proportion between those sowing in places where the harvest has not yet emerged and those training and partnering with nationals to accelerate the harvest where the gospel has been proclaimed in abundance? Should we neglect new, emerging opportunities to maintain historical commitments? To what extent should we give priority to established work and immediately see results if it means forfeiting the long-range potential in new fields where people groups are becoming accessible? These choices are not about what is right or wrong but about determining an appropriate balance and a commitment to what most effectively reaches the whole world.

If you had to make these decisions, which approach would you take?

_____

_____

Missionaries also struggle with the tension between moving or indefinitely staying in a location. Longevity usually guarantees greater results locally. However, working with an exit plan actually produces more effective training of local believers and new national leaders. In addition, missionaries can cover more territory in successive or multiple assignments.

Every generation of IMB missionaries and each successive era of leadership has been committed to fulfilling God's calling and seizing the current opportunity to reach a lost world through the most effective and relevant strategies. We would be foolish to continue doing things as they have always been done without recognizing that the world is changing and that each generation is confronted with new opportunities and potential that did not previously exist. We must put every decision into perspective and focus on our purpose, the vision of an evangelized world, and what it will take to reach all peoples.

> Think about and be prepared to discuss how each of the following ministries can be used to contribute to evangelism and church planting overseas.
> - An agriculturist training farmers to improve production
> - A public-health worker providing pure drinking water and sanitation
> - A teacher conducting English lessons in a university
> - An athlete coaching sports teams
> - An accountant providing financial management for fellow missionaries
> - A businessman conducting seminars on management in developing countries

DAY 3
RESPONDING TO HUMANITARIAN NEEDS

World events and natural disasters often open areas previously closed or resistant to the gospel. Responding to tragedies and chronic suffering allows God's love to be demonstrated through compassionate ministries.

THE IMB REACTS TO IMMEDIATE NEEDS

Following the 2004 tsunami, Christians went to help the eight Asian nations affected. Southern Baptists contributed more than $16 million to help the people of that region rebuild their lives. As hundreds of volunteers worked to dig graves, transport bodies, supply health care, distribute food, rebuild homes, help in resettlement camps, and provide counseling, they reflected Christ in some of the most resistant and closed areas of the world. Relationships built through the response of missionaries and volunteer teams continue to have an impact on the survivors.

Is there a biblical precedent for helping relieve hunger in another part of the world? Read Acts 11:27-30. Briefly explain what happened.

_____

In the 1970s Southern Baptists established a World Hunger Fund in response to a famine in Ethiopia. These offerings and relief efforts, which are made in response to floods, earthquakes, droughts, and other disasters, have significantly contributed to the spread of the gospel. Because IMB administration and Southern Baptist missionaries are already fully supported by the Cooperative Program and the Lottie Moon Christmas Offering® for International Missions, 100 percent of the offerings to world hunger goes to this ministry without any being diverted for administration or promotion. No other organization can make such a claim.

What percentage of money given to the Southern Baptist World Hunger Fund goes into projects to alleviate the suffering of hungry people around the world? _____

Do you or does your church participate in the World Hunger Fund?
❑ Yes   ❑ No

When Hurricane Mitch roared across Honduras in 1998, Southern Baptists responded with more than two million pounds of food, blankets, and clothing. Medical workers came to treat the survivors. More than two thousand volunteers worked through the IMB to build six hundred cinder-block houses across the ravaged country.

Max Furr, an IMB missionary who was the disaster-response coordinator for our relief efforts at the time, said, "In dealing with the physical needs of the people, we were also able to deal with their spiritual needs. We encountered an openness for the gospel never before seen in Honduras." Although thousands lost their lives, thousands more found eternal life. The relief efforts resulted in planting 78 Baptist churches across the country. In one of the hardest-hit areas, eight hundred decisions for Christ were recorded.

Have you participated in a Southern Baptist relief effort?   ❑ Yes   ❑ No
If not, what skills could you contribute to such an effort?

_____

THE ROLE OF AGRICULTURAL ASSISTANCE

Mission opportunities do not arise only from natural disasters. Some are precipitated by conditions that develop slowly. Population pressure in developing nations forces people to farm land once considered unsuitable for agriculture. Hillsides and mountainsides are stripped of trees and natural cover to plant crops. Because of the steep slopes, the topsoil quickly erodes, sending silt into rivers and streams, resulting in barren, unproductive land. Fish disappear, wildlife vanishes, productivity decreases, and people go hungry.

In 1971 Harold Watson, an IMB missionary to the Philippines, began addressing this problem while encouraging church growth. On the island of Mindanao he opened a research and demonstration farm called the Rural Life Center and developed a program called SALT, which stands for Sloping Agricultural Land Technology. This program uses technology to help hungry upland farmers stop soil erosion and grow more food.

Farmers use a simple device to measure the slope of a hillside and determine where to plant fast-growing trees. The trees, planted inches apart across a hillside, replenish the soil with nitrogen as they form hedgerows. Hillside erosion fills in the gaps between the hedgerows and forms flat, natural terraces of rich, productive soil that can be farmed. This simple technology can easily be understood and replicated. Over the years a number of programs were developed to train people in these techniques. All of the programs combined agricultural training with Bible training. "Our ambition," said Watson, "was not only to help someone grow more corn. Our vision from the beginning was also to make a better farmer a better Christian."

Another program called TEACH (Tribal Evangelism, Agriculture, Church, and Health care) has spread the influence and witness of the Rural Life Center into remote areas. Within five years of starting these programs, 20 churches formed in the area around the center. Since then more than 130 have been started, and about 30 percent of the 1,700 Baptist churches on Mindanao are now led by graduates of the Rural Life Center training programs. The techniques Watson pioneered are now used across Asia and beyond, in places like Indonesia, Vietnam, Mexico, India, and Nepal. Agricultural ministries have been replicated all over the world.

EVANGELISM IS THE GOAL

Medical work, humanitarian efforts, agricultural projects, and educational ministries could be carried out as ends in themselves. But missionaries who are involved in such enterprises are motivated by God's call to share more than agricultural techniques or relief to those who suffer. They go because of a desire greater than merely addressing humanitarian needs. Something more than healing sick bodies, improving the quality of life, and advancing the educational level in third-world countries compels them. They go so that all peoples will have an opportunity to know Jesus and so that God's kingdom can be advanced to the ends of the earth.

In your daily work routine do you have opportunities to reflect Christ or present a verbal witness? ❑ Yes ❑ No Would you be more likely to share the good news if you worked in another country? ❑ Yes ❑ No

What conversation starters can you use that would lead to opportunities to witness?

_____

_____

Kingdom growth has a narrow and singular objective; yet it involves comprehensive strategies and diverse gifts for evangelizing the lost, discipling believers, planting and developing churches, training leaders, and ministering to people in need.

A missionary assigned to community development in west Africa recently put this into perspective. With a doctorate in public health, he told how entire villages had been rehabilitated by their programs, which included providing pure drinking water, improving sanitation, and educating the people about nutrition and health. After recounting statistics and describing the community impact he had seen, he began to weep. Sobbing, he said, "We have accomplished all our objectives this term, but I have been a failure because none of these people have trusted in Christ, and healthy in hell doesn't count for much." He expressed the driving passion behind all missionaries, regardless of their roles. Why would we help meet the needs of lost people in this life and neglect to prepare them for eternity?

Circle *T* or *F* to identify the following statements as true or false.

T F 1. There is a conflict between social ministries and evangelism.

T F 2. Missionaries should minister to human needs only where people are open to hear and respond to the gospel.

T F 3. Relief efforts in response to a disaster or chronic human needs are valid Christian ministries as ends in themselves.

T F 4. The IMB is interested only in church planting and therefore doesn't engage in humanitarian work.

T F 5. While social ministries are worthwhile as ends in themselves, they often open the door to opportunities to share the gospel.

T F 6. Helping people in times of need without discrimination demonstrates Christ's love.

DAY 4
GAINING CREATIVE ACCESS

Many missionaries of a former era went to open fields as doctors, teachers, and agriculturists to meet needs and to share the gospel. In a similar way, the professional credentials and experience of many who are called today allow them as teachers, doctors, businessmen, and social workers to plant their lives in places where other missionaries would not be allowed.

CREATING OPPORTUNITIES TO WITNESS

Many who use their gifts and training as a platform to gain entry and provide a witness in restricted countries cannot be openly identified as missionaries, nor can they be linked with the IMB. Identifying them would not only jeopardize their continuing presence, causing them to forfeit their witness and ministry, but in some cases could also endanger the lives of local believers. These personnel provide a vital service in meeting the community's needs—a benefit desired by officials in developing nations.

Almost every country opens its doors to some type of foreign residents. The challenge is discovering skills that are needed and the type of foreign individuals who are acceptable. Open preaching and witnessing may be prohibited, but many live as incarnational witnesses before friends and neighbors. Those relationships invariably lead to opportunities to give an explanation and verbal witness of the gospel. The Holy Spirit, who indwells the message of the gospel, begins to draw hearts to embrace faith in Jesus Christ. Opportunities emerge for nurturing new believers in their faith and in their understanding of the Bible. Cultivating groups of inquirers to come together for mutual strength and encouragement leads to planting churches. In this way a nucleus of witness is established in places where the gospel has not been known.

Creative access: *An approach for discovering and meeting needs so that Christian compassion and witness may result in an opportunity for people to understand and accept the gospel*

Read Acts 18:3. What skill allowed Paul to travel from country to country?

_____

Read Acts 9:23-25. Did Paul have to operate secretly in some of these places?   ❑ Yes   ❑ No

Some would challenge the ethics of a covert witness, saying that missionaries should go only where they are welcome and can openly witness. However, these missionaries don't slip into the country during the night or wear camouflage to hide their identities. They legally enter the country and serve with integrity. Refusing to go would express a shallow level of obedience to our Lord, who told us to disciple all nations. It belittles the lostness of people without access to the gospel and disregards our responsibility to "preach the gospel to the whole creation" (Mark 16:15). It also fails to recognize the sense in which every Christian is to be a missionary.

Certainly some are called to a cross-cultural missionary role, but must that be restricted to preachers and evangelists? If we are all to be witnesses where we live within our community, among our co-workers, and around those with whom we interact as we shop and handle routine business, shouldn't we do that overseas as well? Is it inappropriate to intentionally seek such opportunities in places that do not have a church on every corner proclaiming the gospel? Our presence may be the only opportunity someone has to hear about Jesus.

Governments that fear that missionaries will proselytize their people still need computer engineers, medical workers, and English teachers from abroad. Shouldn't Christians be willing to respond to those requests? If Christians are allowed to enter restricted nations in professional roles, shouldn't the IMB facilitate the filling of these needs by qualified individuals?

The early disciples were sent into a hostile environment where their witness was not welcomed by the local religious authorities or by the Roman political regime. They were threatened and arrested; some were eventually martyred for sharing the gospel.

> Read Acts 4:16-20. How did Peter and John respond when they were ordered not to speak or teach in the name of Jesus—just like many missionary personnel serving in the Muslim world today?

WHATEVER IT TAKES

The privilege of knowing Jesus' salvation should compel us to do whatever it takes to share Him with others. We should be willing to endure ridicule, to risk repercussions, and even to place ourselves in danger so that others can have the opportunity to know Jesus.

> Read Philippians 1:12-13. What unique circumstances gave Paul an opportunity to witness? What resulted?

In His final exhortation to His followers, Jesus expressed the passion and urgency of extending His kingdom to the ends of the earth. He did not say to go and make disciples wherever it is safe and legal to do so. He did not qualify His instructions to witness only where you are welcome. Jesus added no contingency clauses; the mandate was all nations and all peoples, regardless! If we accept Jesus' unqualified mandate, we should consider no country closed to the gospel. Places where a missionary presence is not allowed and people have not had access to the gospel are sometimes called the Last Frontier of the Great Commission.

Last Frontier: *Unreached people groups (less than 2 percent evangelical Christians) with little or no access to the gospel, in which there have been no new evangelical church starts within the past two years*

Cambodia is a beautiful country in Indochina. In the early 1990s Indochina was still under Communist rule and a restricted missionary presence. But following the reign of Pol Pot and the Khmer Rouge—and the tragic genocide that killed or displaced millions—Cambodia was destitute. Several social workers entered this foreboding environment with a nongovernment humanitarian agency. They provided medical care, improved sanitation, and helped create better working conditions in the factories. Others joined the team to install water-purification equipment, design systems for sewage disposal, rebuild schools, and contribute to educational programs. They carried out their assignments professionally and won the favor of government and community officials.

Within two years 24 house churches had emerged in the capital city of Phnom Penh. Two years later a nationwide Baptist convention was formed with 43 organized churches. Five years later there were more than 200 Baptist churches. This didn't happen through missionary church planters who blitzed the country in an open witness but through national believers who shared their faith. They were trained and encouraged by missionaries whose diversity of skills and assignments allowed them to enter the country. They seized the opportunity for an incarnational presence and witness by providing a value-added service to a country and people in need.

Match the following roles and strategies that are related to the Last Frontier with the correct definitions.

___ 1. Restricted access

___ 2. Creative access

___ 3. Platforms

___ 4. Itinerant missionaries

a. Missionaries who travel in and out of countries where they are not allowed to reside permanently

b. Meeting an acceptable need of a country or society in order to live in a place where missionaries are not allowed

c. Places where missionaries are not allowed and other roles must be found for taking the gospel to the people

d. Using vocational experience and skills to gain entry to a country and share the gospel

DAY 5

THE CHALLENGE OF THE REMAINING TASK

We have noted that God is moving in providence and power as the 21st century progresses. Missionaries are being assigned to places that would have been unthinkable just a few years ago. They are serving in China, the former Soviet Union, eastern Europe, and Muslim countries. Church-planting movements are accelerating the spread of the gospel. For several years missionaries have reported that more than one thousand new believers are being baptized each day, and in 2003 the number of converts exceeded half a million for the first time.

THE TASK THAT REMAINS

The most important indication of advance may be the fact that IMB missionaries engaged 146 previously unreached people groups in 2002 and touched 131 more new people groups for the first time in 2003. Many other people groups are being reached by other mission groups. However, the challenge remains of reaching all peoples. There is still a gap of lostness among many who have not yet heard the gospel, as well as those who have had the opportunity to hear but have not responded to follow Jesus as Savior and Lord.

Check any of the following circumstances that justify our not proclaiming
the gospel to a Last Frontier nation or people group.
❑ The government prohibits proselytizing by missionaries.
❑ Danger prevents foreigners from living in the country.
❑ Local believers could be persecuted and even killed.
❑ We must respect laws that forbid sharing a Christian witness.
❑ We might be arrested or deported for sharing our faith.

I hope you did not find a single exception. Although the task of evangelization still remains, priority is being given to people groups and strategic population segments with 100,000 or more that have no Christian witness. This category still includes 511 people groups, 61 with a population of more than one million.

Thousands of smaller micro-people groups do not have access to the gospel in their own languages and cultures. We have little hope of having enough missionaries to reach all of them. We would have to double the number of missionaries to have just one person assigned to each people group. But if 43,000 Southern Baptist churches were mobilized and caught a vision for involvement and thousands of volunteers assisted, the task could be achieved.

In addition to the unengaged people groups that have no witness, over four thousand more are unreached. These may be countries or people groups that have a Christian witness and even some churches; but fewer than 2 percent of the people have been evangelized in terms of hearing the gospel, and no effective, multiplying church growth or witness is occurring that would expand access to the gospel. Therefore, at least 98 percent of the people are unreached.

As research was able to identify the sections of the world that had not been evangelized and specific people groups that had not responded or had not even had an opportunity to hear the gospel, it became possible also to identify why these were unreached. To a large extent it has been because missionary efforts have not yet expanded to them.

Where are the unengaged and unreached people groups? Look at a world
map or globe as you read the following paragraph.

Unreached people groups are found in every region of the world. Almost half of the unengaged people groups with 100,000 people or more are found among the massive population of south Asia. Many of those still unreached are in former Communist countries and throughout the Muslim world, especially in northern Africa, the Middle East, and the central-Asian republics. West Africa has one of the largest numbers of unreached people groups, but 75 percent of the 1,100 unevangelized groups in that region are smaller tribes with fewer than 15,000 people.

THE CHALLENGE OF ORAL CULTURES

We have discovered that the reason many unengaged people groups have not heard the gospel is that they are oral cultures. Basically illiterate, they could not read the Bible or Christian literature even if it were available. They may be near neighbors or may even live in the midst of others who have been evangelized, but the gospel has not penetrated their understanding in their language and in the oral, narrative way they receive and understand information.

Oral cultures represent 1.5 billion people and a majority of the unengaged people groups. For example, approximately 65 percent of the men and 85 percent of the women in Islamic cultures are exclusively oral communicators. Most of the unreached animistic tribes are illiterate. There are still 4,147 languages that have no Scripture and at least 1,000 more that do not have the Bible or New Testament, though a portion of Scripture may exist in their language.

God is not just interested in the world as a whole, but He knows and loves each individual. One of the Aukaners God loves is Don, a man of great influence in his village. We introduced Don to God's Word through a method called chronological Bible storying. Don listened to tapes in which an Aukaner told foundational Bible stories from the creation to Christ's ascension. After repeated hearings, he asked, "Do you believe God can speak to you in a dream?" We said yes. He then began to tell us of his recurring dream since listening to the Bible stories.

"In my dream I'm in the front of my canoe, and my wife is in the back as we paddle down the river. All of a sudden I look into the clouds and see Jesus standing. He calls me by name and says, 'Come.' So I paddle over to the shore and follow the path leading to Jesus. I turn around, and my wife, children, and much of my village are following as well. What do you think that means?"

With joy we told Don that God was calling him to a relationship with Jesus Christ, and when he chose to follow Christ, he was going to lead much of his family and others to follow Him as well.

What a God we serve! He found an unlikely man in a remote village and called him by name![2]

—VICKI, MIDDLE AMERICA AND THE CARIBBEAN

Oral cultures: *People within a given society or culture who best understand their world through spoken stories*

Chronological Bible storying: *A method of evangelizing, discipling, and training a people by relating to them, in a culturally suitable manner, the great stories of the Bible from creation to redemption to Christ's return*

Chronological Bible storying has been used to share the gospel, but these people groups also need discipleship and training for church planting to take place. Several mission agencies, including the IMB, have sought to engage oral cultures and people groups. Working together, these agencies have developed oral materials for discipleship and leadership training that are based on the narrative approach of chronological Bible storying. Through this partnership duplication is avoided, the provision of materials for people groups all over the world is accelerated, and other mission agencies are served by these cooperative efforts.

Are you a good storyteller?　❑ Yes　❑ No
Do you know many of the stories in the Bible?　❑ Yes　❑ No
Do you feel this approach may be your strength?　❑ Yes　❑ No
Pray with an open mind about how God might use you and fellow believers in reaching illiterate or oral learners.

While the remaining challenge is formidable, progress is being made. Every country in the world has been penetrated with the gospel. Unreached people groups are systematically being evangelized. We know where the gaps exist, and Jesus assured us that one day the gospel would be proclaimed in the whole world as a witness to all peoples. The Apostle John envisioned in Revelation 7:9 when that day would come. He saw a multitude from every nation, tribe, people, and language represented around God's throne.

The following paragraph includes reasons the gospel has not yet reached entire people groups. Underline them.

The primary barrier to finishing the task may not be culture, language, lack of Scripture, religious resistance, or government restrictions but our lack of obedience and devotion to the task. In our churches indifference to the Great Commission and the tendency to give mission organizations low priority are depriving a lost world of the gospel. Multitudes may remain in darkness because of our unwillingness to hear God's call, offer our lives for His service, or give and provide the resources needed for sending and supporting more missionaries. We are stewards of the gospel, called to obedience and commissioned to disciple all peoples.

As you think about each reason many people groups remain unreached, which ones can you or your church overcome to obey God's call?

_____

_____

_____

_____

1. Mark Kelly, "Gospel Multiplies Among India's Lingayat People So Much That Coordinators May Leave," Baptist Press [online], 2 December 2005 [cited 9 January 2006]. Available from the Internet: *www.bpnews.net.*
2. "He calls me by name," *Voices of the Faithful,* comp. Kim P. Davis (Brentwood, TN: Integrity Publishers, 2005), 12. Name changed for security reasons.

WEEK 5
CHURCH-PLANTING MOVEMENTS

VERSE TO REMEMBER

"You are the body of Christ,
and each one of you is a part of it."
1 CORINTHIANS 12:27, NIV

Since Oliver and his wife, Joy, began mentoring six Chinese believers less than two years ago, those believers have started more than 55 churches and have led four thousand people to Christ. The conversions keep coming so fast that it's impossible to keep count. But Oliver is clear about one thing: he didn't start it—God did. And He's worked primarily through Chinese believers, which is the foundation of a lasting church-planting movement. "God's in the driver's seat," Oliver says. "God was working [here] since the beginning, and He asked us to show up."[1]

Someone has said, "If you don't know where you are going, any road will do." However, if we know where we want to go, we must take the right road. Strategic planning not only identifies the road to take but also determines the use of budget resources and missionary deployment. This week you will learn the strategy behind many current mission practices so that you and your church can wisely contribute to this effort to plant churches that make the gospel accessible to all people.

DAY 1
PLANTING REPRODUCING CHURCHES

One of my most thrilling travel experiences was the privilege of visiting Cambodia for the first time. I made the trip right after the fifth annual meeting of the Cambodian Baptist Convention. At the time it reported 243 churches with a total of more than 16,000 baptized members. None of the churches were led by missionaries. In fact, if foreigners had even attended the churches, they would have jeopardized their security in this Communist country.

The missionaries engaged in humanitarian projects and poured themselves into discipling and training lay leaders who not only led their own congregations but also started others. I attended one of the two-week training sessions attended by 20 lay pastors. Most of them had been believers for fewer than two years. Each reported pastoring at least two churches; one of the men pastored six. All of them had projected locations for starting new churches as soon as their training was finished.

CHURCHES STARTING CHURCHES

The objective of a church-planting strategy of evangelism is more than an increase in the number of churches. Planting new churches is the surest way to increase the number of believers. But missionaries themselves cannot produce a rapid multiplication of new churches. The strategy depends on churches starting churches. The churches must catch the vision of the missionary or national church planter to extend their witness and to nurture believers in another location.

Church planting occurs when a single church is started. A church-growth movement occurs when several churches are started and begin other churches. For a church-planting movement to occur, a spiritual element must be present in a new church's DNA. One church starts another, which starts another. Two churches become 4, 4 become 8, and 8 become 16 in rapid, exponential multiplication.

Describe the distinctions among the following terms.

Church planting: _____

Church growth: _____

Church-planting movements: _____

In one country where local Baptists have caught the vision of church-planting movements, a new congregation cannot be recognized as an organized member church of the convention until it has started another mission. During a church-planting movement in a Latin American country, the number of churches increased from 100 to 1,340 in approximately 10 years, and the number of members grew sevenfold.

A Church-Planting Movement in Latin America

In India there were 28 Baptist churches among a people group numbering 90 million. No new church had been started in 25 years because the churches had focused on a model that depended on outsiders contributing resources to provide a building and support their pastors. When these subsidies were discontinued, they ceased to grow. But then they began to get a renewed fervor for evangelism through the training and influence of a missionary. They began to realize that a church's biblical and spiritual nature was contingent neither on a full-time, seminary-trained pastor nor on special facilities. New congregations of believers began to emerge and multiply.

During the next two years 14 new churches were started. Three years later there were 547 churches, which then more than doubled. Currently, there are more than 2,900 Baptist churches among this people group. These churches are not just small cells of two or three believers or an extended family meeting together for worship. A recent research report indicated that the average number of baptized members meeting regularly for worship was more than 60 in each church.

Church-planting movements are taking place throughout China as house-church networks multiply in phenomenal numbers. Already three such networks report 18 million to 20 million members, each one larger than the Southern Baptist Convention. An International Mission

Board strategy coordinator went to a province with three churches in 1993, and by 1998 there were 550 churches.

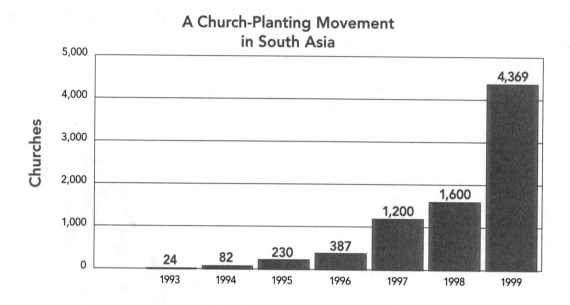

Presently, the IMB is tracking about 80 existing and potential church-planting movements throughout the world. Many more are beginning to emerge. Incremental growth reported in the past has turned into church-growth rates of more than 20 percent a year. In 2001 8,379 new churches were started. That number grew to more than 16,600 the following year, and 21,028 were started in 2003. This is not an aberration or a short-lived peak in church planting. In addition to these new churches, 50,297 additional mission points and outreach groups that are not yet churches are being reported—an indication that the movement will continue.

This pace of new church growth was the primary factor in being able to report more than 600,000 new believers baptized overseas for the first time in the history of the IMB. New churches invariably grow faster and reach more people than older, established churches do.

FOLLOWING THE NEW TESTAMENT MODEL

A church is a group of baptized believers drawn together by the Holy Spirit into a covenant fellowship for the purpose of worship, fellowship, witness, nurture, and ministry. The biblical model of the church in Acts 2:46-47 describes the first house churches. They did not require a building or specially trained leadership from outside the congregation itself. Witness began to expand spontaneously. Groups of believers met together, and new churches began to emerge.

Church: *A group of baptized believers drawn together by the Holy Spirit into a covenant fellowship for the purpose of worship, fellowship, witness, nurture, and ministry*

Check the elements that are essential for a church to exist. Be prepared to give a biblical teaching or example for each element that you check.

❏ 1. A specific building as a place of worship apart from one's home

❏ 2. An ordained, seminary-trained pastor

❏ 3. At least 15 baptized members

❏ 4. Must gather for worship on Sunday, the first day of the week

❏ 5. A group of baptized believers gathered into a fellowship for worship and witness

❏ 6. Must be a covenant community with a self-identity as a church

❏ 7. Must have a constitution and by-laws and be chartered by another recognized church

DAY 2
FACTORS LEADING TO A CHURCH-PLANTING MOVEMENT

What are the factors that enable a church-planting movement to occur? Scripture and worship must be in the heart language of the people. This heart language eliminates cross-cultural and other barriers to worship. Hearing the gospel allows the church to multiply within a homogeneous people group.

LEADERS FOR CHURCHES

Churches that rapidly multiply usually have bivocational lay pastors and leaders. They emerge from within the congregation and give evidence of spiritual gifts and sensitivity for leadership roles. They are not limited by a lack of financial support or educational degrees. They can readily train others, multiplying the leadership that is needed.

However, the rapid evangelistic growth does not necessarily happen because of leaders. The real catalyst is new believers who enthusiastically share their faith person to person wherever they can. The movement often starts when the gospel is introduced for the first time by a Western or national missionary, but lay leaders quickly emerge.

Most missionaries involved in church-planting movements practice Paul's admonition to Timothy in 2 Timothy 2:2. Record the four steps of training:

(1) _____ taught (2) _____, who was to pass on the teaching to (3) _____, who were to teach (4) _____.

Church-planting movements are taking place among previously unreached people groups, even when restrictions on preaching, conducting public worship, and witnessing abound. Many testimonies reflect that an evangelist or a missionary has found a "man of peace" (Luke 10:6, NIV), as Jesus instructed His disciples when He sent them out. This person of influence has an important contact in the community who may or may not become a believer. Yet he opens the door to relationships that allow the gospel to be shared.

The initial witness and the first churches started should be not only indigenous but also firmly grounded on the authority of the Bible and the priesthood of all believers. Media missionaries working outside the country have often played a vital role in saturating the area with gospel radio broadcasts and in providing the *Jesus* film in forms that can be distributed and shared from household to household.

One remote area in a restricted, closed country has seen 1,800 believers come to Christ over the past five years through literature and video packets strategically dropped throughout the area. These brick-sized packets, containing the *Jesus* film, a New Testament in the local language, and other evangelistic literature, were found and passed from family to family and house to house. The villagers talked about what they had seen and read. They not only believed the gospel but also shared it in a widespread witness.

Strategies like this are often implemented among people groups among whom a missionary cannot live. After discovering ways to plant the gospel through saturation witnessing, an external missionary nurtures the movement by providing leadership training, conducting workshops on evangelism and discipleship, and mobilizing prayer support.

Read Acts 14:23. Paul had been in each city on his first missionary journey for only two or three weeks. Whom did he appoint or ordain in each church?

_____

Where did these leaders come from? _____

Did he have trust and confidence primarily in the leaders' ability? ❑ Yes ❑ No

A FOUR-STEP APPROACH

In places where it is possible to live among the people or at least visit the area periodically, the missionary follows a four-step approach of modeling, assisting, watching, and leaving. He may lead the first group of believers for a few weeks, but he leads in such a way that a local leader can assume that responsibility. After receiving encouragement, training, and assistance for a short time, the local leader can imitate the method and pass on the training to other lay pastors and evangelists. Relinquishing all leadership roles, the missionary stays in contact, watching and advising as needed before leaving and moving on to other unevangelized areas.

Another missionary has identified principles for nurturing church-planting movements with the acrostic POUCH, which stands for Participative Bible study and worship, Obedience to God's Word, Unpaid and multiple lay leaders, Cell churches that rapidly divide and multiply, and Homes as the primary meeting place in a community where outsiders feel welcome.

> Read 1 Corinthians 16:19. Why did Paul send greetings
> to Priscilla and Aquila?
> ❏ They had settled their argument.
> ❏ They had worked hard for the Lord.
> ❏ They led a house church.
> ❏ They had risked their lives for Paul.

In Acts 18:24-28 Priscilla and Aquila trained a novice preacher, who in turn became an effective leader in Achaia. Meanwhile, the couple continued their ministry in Ephesus.

The reluctance to relinquish leadership early in the process, if not from the very beginning, has been one of the primary weaknesses of traditional church-planting efforts. Once the missionary becomes accepted as the primary leader, he feels awkward trying to pass on that role to an untrained leader within the group. If the new church looks for a pastor from outside the congregation, it assumes the burden of financial support. Funding his salary then imposes another weakness. Raising money becomes detrimental to the strength and vitality of the church, impeding its ability to grow and multiply spontaneously and independently.

Obviously, only God can start a church-planting movement. This spiritual movement affirms the power of the gospel to change lives and spreads through the fervent witness of new believers. Implementing prescribed methods and following certain steps do not guarantee that a church-planting movement will occur. God, in His providence, chooses to move in His timing in certain places and among certain peoples. But we can learn how to cooperate with God in His divine activity, knowing that He desires everyone to repent and come to the knowledge of the truth.

Many elements are essential to a church-planting movement. List three.

1. _____

2. _____

3. _____

Would it be possible for your church to plant new churches in your community?   ❑ Yes   ❑ No   Explain why or why not.

_____

_____

DAY 3
PRODUCING INDIGENOUS RESULTS

Most churches in America would not serve as models for churches in other countries. Many traditional churches grow to the point of having to provide special facilities and programs. When a congregation grows, it tends to place greater attention on its own internal needs than on starting new churches and missionary outreach.

THE VALUE OF INDIGENOUS CHURCHES

Rapidly multiplying churches must be indigenous. This means no church can depend on outside finances and leadership. From the beginning it must be self-supporting, self-governing under the lordship of Christ, and self-propagating in extending its witness. It must practice an expression of organization and worship that is consistent with biblical teaching but in its own cultural context. It should be able to provide its own facilities for worship and support its own pastors, often bivocational lay leaders who emerge from within the congregation.

In the past we have asked people to cross ethnic, language, and geographic barriers to become like our churches here. Churches built on Western models seldom multiply and usually cannot even survive unless someone props them up with an artificial system of support.

A lesson in landscaping illustrates this principle. I would like to have palm trees and tropical shrubs in my yard like the ones I enjoyed in Indonesia and see when I go to Florida. But because these plants are not indigenous to my part of the country, they would not survive on their own apart from a greenhouse environment.

As we noted in day 2, Scripture and worship should always be in the heart language of the people. Also, the gospel must be communicated in their own cultural context. Church-planting movements are the only way the gospel can spread spontaneously and provide all people access to the message of saving faith in Christ. Rapidly multiplying congregations are the only way a massive number of new believers can be discipled and nurtured in their faith. Therefore, the IMB's mission strategies must facilitate this movement.

> Note the radical and spontaneous growth of the New Testament church in the Book of Acts. Write what is said about the churches in the following passages.
>
> Acts 5:42: _____
>
> Acts 9:31: _____
>
> Acts 16:5: _____

COMMON FACTORS IN SUCCESSFUL CHURCH PLANTING

Several common factors have been identified in places where indigenous churches are multiplying rapidly. *The vitality and prominence of prayer* in the missionary's life and in the lives of the new believers and their leaders are evident. Prayer is the source of power for evangelistic harvest and subsequent church growth. Often we at the IMB discover a prayer network of churches and partners abroad who have adopted a people group and have fervently interceded and prayed for the people.

Another element is *abundant sowing of the gospel*. Saturation of the gospel always precedes church growth. It would be a presumptuous mistake to think that one missionary or team can implement church-planting methods without extensive evangelistic witnessing, sometimes for years. Media tools, Bible and literature distribution, verbal proclamation, and personal witness can all be used effectively. The method is not as important as the conviction that God indwells the message and truth of the gospel, and He will draw people to faith in Christ. There is no substitute for scriptural authority in a church-planting movement.

In my earlier years of church planting, as groups of new believers came together and churches were formed, I became frustrated by one aspect of the Great Commission. Jesus instructed us to teach them "'to observe everything I have commanded you'" (Matt. 28:20). New Christians usually had no background for understanding anything related to the Bible, the church, and the Christian way of life. I had spent my time introducing Jesus' claims and cultivating their understanding and acceptance of the plan of salvation. As they came to the point of commitment and obedience in baptism, I began to contemplate what I should teach them first. What was the most important priority? What was the next most important lesson they should learn as new Christians? As I outlined all of the essentials that Jesus taught, I began to realize that it would take years to cover these lessons when I met with each church once a week.

We had already made Bibles available, and the believers were reading them diligently. Following baptism, the task of making disciples involved teaching them that the Bible is the true, revealed Word of God. They were to read it, study it, meditate on it, and believe it. They were to follow its instructions and teachings. From that context I came to understand that believers who rapidly multiply and share their faith are those who accept and follow the authority of God's Word for all matters of faith and practice. Jesus was saying to me, "Teach them obedience."

Another element in the success of indigenous churches is *intentional church planting*. Churches don't just happen. What is done in evangelism and ministry should be done in a way that enables new believers to form congregations. Then local lay leaders and churches meet in facilities that they themselves provide.

In one restrictive country where a limited number of churches existed, the authorities refused to allow any new churches to be built or started. They said, "You Christians will just have to meet in your homes." The historically slow growth of these established churches literally exploded, with hundreds of house churches spreading in every village and community. Now everyone is in close proximity to a church, and the informal home setting makes it conducive for unsaved neighbors to attend and hear the gospel.

The size, venue, and functioning of house churches may be similar to cell groups, but churches that rapidly multiply are not part of a megachurch or a centralized ecclesiastical identity. Each one is independent and autonomous. House churches grow by multiplying and starting other groups from their evangelistic efforts. Indigenous churches are not ingrown but focus on starting new congregations.

What are four characteristics of an indigenous church?

1. _____

2. _____

3. _____

4. _____

Contrast this model with your church. Does your church have an intentional model for planting new churches on an ongoing basis?   ❑ Yes   ❑ No

DAY 4
AVOIDING HELP THAT HURTS

Our mission efforts must result in churches that can exist, grow, and multiply within their own cultures and economies without dependence on foreign resources. Otherwise, we place an obstacle in the way of church planting and multiplication that may surprise you.

DOES HELP SOMETIMES HURT?

We are in an era of increased involvement in international missions. Partnerships and volunteer projects take many Southern Baptists overseas, where they are confronted by poverty and economic disparity. We commend their compassionate desire to help believers and churches. But many well-meaning people seek to help these churches in a way that actually hurts them spiritually and inhibits their effectiveness and growth. A new ministry can degenerate because of material assistance that inhibits the church's health and growth.

Read Acts 18:2-4. How was Paul supported as he traveled from church to church?

Many years of missionary work around the world have taught us that it is a mistake to try to accelerate growth through the infusion of financial aid to build churches and support pastors. Well-intended financial assistance too often creates dependence and handicaps the initiative and faith that are essential to growth. It creates a patronizing welfare mentality on the part of local believers. Potential growth often stalls because local people are led to believe that it can't be done unless an overseas benefactor provides the funds.

When that happens, the congregation loses a sense of ownership and ceases to be responsible and conscientious stewards because others are providing the financial needs of their pastor and the church. Those who develop a pipeline of support from the United States through their contacts with volunteers and others breed jealousy among those who do not receive such aid. Cooperation among churches may diminish since they no longer have to work together in mutual support, encouragement, and interdependency.

The donor lives under the illusion of assisting just until the church can become self-supporting, but that seldom happens. People are deprived of the opportunity to grow in faith, learning to depend on God and discovering that He is sufficient for all of their needs. Financial subsidies from abroad also reinforce and propagate a Western model of a church that sees a building and a paid pastor as essential rather than encouraging a reproducible biblical model of the church as gathered believers responsible for their own leadership and facilities.

In addition, the work of missionaries is often undercut. They are seen as uncaring in not providing the same material and financial aid that volunteers and churches in the United States are willing to provide. Often, indigenous churches grow to call and support a full-time pastor and build worship facilities, but when they have been self-supporting from the beginning, they are the result of spiritual vitality and growth, not vice versa.

List reasons that providing ongoing financial support for churches overseas is detrimental to their health and growth.

HOW OUTSIDE AID INHIBITS A CHURCH-PLANTING MOVEMENT

Multitudes of national church planters are being supported from abroad to start churches, especially where there is a shortage of Western missionaries. Many prominent mission agencies promote the support of national pastors and evangelists on the basis that they are cheaper than Western missionaries. Supposedly, they are more effective since they don't have to learn a new language and can serve in their own culture. The IMB trains more than 120,000 national workers each year; nationals are the key to an indigenous church-planting strategy. But the IMB's national workers depend on local support, not the support of the IMB.

Even national workers find it difficult to avoid creating dependency when they become the primary leader. Their ministries may not survive without the support of local congregations. Generally, church growth plateaus or ceases when others are hired to do the work. Being neither a national evangelist nor a cross-cultural Western missionary guarantees effectiveness or success. The determining factor is whether one has the anointing of God's Holy Spirit.

The explosive growth of the church in China never would have occurred if dependency on missionary societies had continued. The highest rate of church growth is occurring in some of poorest countries. Baptists in Malawi started almost one church for every two already organized in a recent year. Bangladesh, where the annual per-capita income is less than one hundred dollars, reports 7,800 new church starts in the past 10 years.

In contrast, growth proceeds slowly where well-meaning supporters from abroad provide financial aid. Some areas of Latin America exhibit all of the conditions for an evangelistic harvest; yet church growth is minimal because of the dependency created by partners from the United States. A few years ago a state convention enthusiastically entered a partnership with an eastern European country. As an element of the partnership, every new church-planting effort was funded by churches in America. They met their goal of starting 20 churches in five years, providing salaries for the church planters and pastors and funding for the church building. Meanwhile, a neighboring country with similar conditions and responsiveness saw more than 200 new churches planted in the same time frame. Churches in the second country are continuing to reproduce because they never depended on foreign subsidies.

In one of the most impoverished, restricted countries in the world, the average salary is equivalent to nine dollars a month. Yet the wind of the Spirit is blowing, with phenomenal numbers of baptisms and church starts. One pastor says that he does not suffer because of what he does not have. He testifies, "Because we have God, we have everything!"

List ways we can contribute to church planting other than financial help.

DAY 5
STRATEGY COORDINATORS LEADING THE WAY

In the past, when missionaries were organized according to the countries in which they resided, their efforts usually focused on the national language and the dominant culture. Some areas received all of the attention and resources, while other vast areas and peoples were neglected. The large mission structures required an inordinate amount of time and resources just to administer the needs of the missionaries themselves. In most instances whole countries are too large and complex to represent a common approach or strategy.

PRESENT STRATEGIES

In contrast to past strategies, field missionaries are now organized in local teams, each one focused on a specific people group or segment of the population. Other support teams provide business-management services for those in a given country or area. Working together, IMB mission teams apply their diversity of gifts and skills to a common task. Most teams include a strategy coordinator, who takes responsibility for leading a team to develop and implement a strategy for a church-planting movement among a specific target group or area. This person is usually an IMB missionary, but in some situations our personnel work under a local national leader or someone with another evangelical agency. This role is not as critical where churches have been planted and Christians are available to reach and evangelize their people. However, a strategy coordinator is essential for making an impact on an unreached people group.

> **Strategy coordinator:** *A missionary who takes responsibility for developing a comprehensive plan aimed at initiating and nurturing a church-planting movement among an unreached people group or population segment*

The coordinator, along with others on the team, engages the people group through direct relationship building, witness, and discipleship. A knowledgeable model of how to present the gospel in the cultural context of the people, he demonstrates a commitment to evangelism and discipleship. He serves as the team leader, facilitating each team member's involvement and use of gifts, along with those of other Great Commission partners.

In addition, the strategy coordinator is responsible for seeing that a prayer network is developed and guides in advocacy for the people group among churches and our Southern Baptist constituency. He networks with other mission agencies and organizations to multiply and accelerate engagement among the people group and to avoid duplication of efforts.

For example, when a strategy coordinator in Central Asia was the only unit assigned to his people group, he was able to make a phenomenal impact by utilizing the services and gifts of others. As a result of his advocacy for his people, Campus Crusade produced and distributed the *Jesus* film in the local language, and TransWorld Radio began evangelistic broadcasts into the country. He facilitated the efforts of Operation Mobilization and Youth with a Mission to sow seeds in the country. Stateside partner churches sent volunteers to teach English as a Second Language. These resources were parts of an intentional strategy.

Someone filling this role is usually innovative, envisioning the end result from a big-picture perspective and figuring out, with God's leadership, how to move from an unreached people group to a church-planting movement. He focuses on research and understanding demographics and cultural nuances. He identifies a "man of peace" (Luke 10:6, NIV), who opens the door to acceptance and credibility in the community. Working with a team of missionary colleagues, he develops a model for training national believers and leaders; his leadership and guidance keep the team in a catalytic role to prevent dependency on outside personnel and resources.

The strategy coordinator is the expert with regard to a people group. He discerns social structures and economic needs that can be used to gain acceptance. He determines and helps mobilize resources for Bible translation, radio broadcasts, literature distribution, prayerwalking, and ministries that meet needs. He works like the foreman in a factory—not always on the front line but creating a synergy among the team that gets the job done. The attitude is not "What can I do?" but "What can I do to lead, enable, and facilitate making the gospel accessible to these people?" This servant role supports and coordinates the work of the team.

What is the significance of the two words used to define this leadership role?

Strategy: _____

Coordinator: _____

THE NEED FOR MORE STRATEGY COORDINATORS

Much of the global advance of the IMB in engaging new people groups is contingent on more missionaries who are gifted and willing to serve as strategy coordinators. Concentrating on specific people groups allows the gospel to be presented within the context of unique cultural distinctions and worldviews and then to spread among a homogeneous population group without encountering barriers of language and ethnic discrimination.

The ability of the IMB to engage more than one thousand new people groups in the past 10 years is primarily due to God's providence and power throughout the world. But strategy coordinators have played a key role in discerning where God is at work, coordinating the team, and leading the effort to plant the gospel. Men and women from every conceivable background have been trained and have stepped into this strategic assignment.

> What ability do you have that would qualify you as a strategy coordinator?
> ❑ Business administrator   ❑ Teacher   ❑ Church worker
> ❑ School administrator   ❑ Professor   ❑ Building contractor
> Other: _____

Strategy coordinators are the primary personnel need in every region. Many missionaries who come from a business or an educational background have found that their experience and training uniquely equip them for this task. Multitudes continue to perish without the gospel as they wait for someone to respond to God's call and say, "I'll be the one."

> Check the reasons you think a strategy coordinator is a critical role.
> ❑ 1. It is essential for someone to do research and understand the culture
>   and the people to be reached.
> ❑ 2. Someone needs the skills to discern the bridges and barriers to making
>   the gospel known in a specific area.
> ❑ 3. A role is needed for missionaries who are not gifted in evangelism
>   and discipleship.
> ❑ 4. Without someone to network and coordinate efforts with other mission
>   groups, conflict, confusion, and duplicated effort would likely result.
> ❑ 5. Each missionary can maximize his or her contribution to the task
>   when someone guides and coordinates the team.
> ❑ 6. In security-sensitive locations someone is needed to serve as
>   an advocate and a point of contact for outside partner entities.
> ❑ 7. This role fills in the organizational structure established by the IMB.
> ❑ 8. Someone needs to mentor and train personnel assigned to the team.

1. "Former Sales Rep Helps Start a 'People Explosion' in China." Baptist Press [online], 9 December 2005 [cited 9 January 2006]. Available from the Internet: *www.bpnews.net*. Names changed for security reasons.

Week 6

SENDING OUT THE CALLED

VERSE TO REMEMBER

" 'I am in them and You are in Me. May they be made
completely one, so the world may know You have sent
Me and have loved them as You have loved me.' "

JOHN 17:23

Mike and Molly Turner serve as strategy coordinators in a capital city in northern Africa, where the majority of people follow Islam. Each week four American women sit among a dozen or so African prostitutes in a circle of mismatched chairs and a couch. The group, led by Molly, includes journeyman Susan and two volunteers. Later in the week they meet together as a house church with their teammates. After a meal and prayer Susan shares from memory the story of God's commanding Abraham to sacrifice his son Isaac. Orally sharing stories helps the missionaries practice for their own ministries, which often involve people who are more accustomed to sharing information orally rather than through the written word.[1]

Only in the past two hundred years—since William Carey went to India—has the modern missionary movement been launched. Initially, missionaries followed on the coattails of 19th-century European colonial expansion. Initial outposts of Christian witness were established only in coastal cities and provinces. Much later groups, such as the African Inland Mission and the China Inland Mission, were devoted to taking the gospel to interior areas. Where will 21st-century missionaries come from? How will they be supported? If you meet a person in the International Service Corps or the Masters Program, will you meet a real missionary? This week you will learn what your church can do to send out the called.

DAY 1
RESPONDING TO GOD'S CALL

Why is the International Mission Board's basic strategy to send and support missionaries when there are so many other things we could do? Why are we essentially a missionary-sending agency? We send because Jesus told us to go! He knew that the personal communication and verbal witness of a Christian living among lost people are the most direct and effective channels for fulfilling our mission.

Many methodologies can take the gospel to a lost world, and we applaud, support, and engage in many of them. The gospel can be broadcast to millions using media. Bibles and literature can be published and distributed. But Jesus did not tell us just to contribute our monetary support or to find the most cost-efficient way of proclaiming the gospel. He said to go and be His witnesses to the ends of the earth.

AN INCARNATIONAL WITNESS

When missionaries or even short-term volunteers plant their lives in a culture among people who do not know Jesus, the living presence of Jesus Himself goes with them. As they live their faith through friendships, people can observe the reality of their relationship with Jesus. Being there, missionaries can communicate with an understanding of the worldview of the people they live among. They can cultivate a witness, follow up, nurture new fellowships of believers, and walk alongside those God calls out as indigenous, local leaders.

Identify two reasons the IMB is primarily a missionary-sending agency.

1. _____

2. _____

We call our approach an incarnational witness. We allow nonbelievers to observe what it means to be a follower of Christ. God revealed Himself to humankind in the same way. Jesus Christ became flesh, enabling the world to behold His glory. We would not presume to approach the uniqueness and significance of Jesus as God incarnate, but the message of Christ is best communicated through the lives of those in whom Christ dwells. Many peoples of the world live in places were no churches exist. They do not have access to God's Word and have never known a Christian. They are best able to see and understand a Christian witness when a believer lives in their midst.

> **Incarnational witness:** *Living in flesh and blood a testimony of our faith so that our behavior and lifestyle are a witness to the people around us. Allowing people to see Jesus in us gives credibility to a verbal witness.*

In your own words, tell what it means to be an incarnational witness.

_____

_____

Recall an experience when God used you as an incarnational witness.

_____

_____

THE IMB'S SENDING PROCESS

As we envision kingdom growth to the ends of the world, how does the IMB select missionaries? Some in our denomination think we should appoint anyone in a Southern Baptist church who feels called to missions without regard to qualifications. Then we should support whatever he or she personally wants to do overseas. The IMB is often criticized for maintaining high standards and criteria in the approval process, although relatively few who apply for missionary service are turned down.

The IMB has retained historic phrasing in documents that list the guidelines for selecting missionary appointees. The IMB is instructed to find, appoint, arrange support for, equip, and send God-called Southern Baptist missionaries "who give evidence of piety, zeal for the Master's kingdom, conviction of truth as held by Baptists, and talents for missionary service."

Write one action that might demonstrate each of the following qualifications for missionary appointment.

1. Piety: _____

2. Zeal for the kingdom: _____

3. Conviction of truth as held by Baptists: _____

_____

4. Talents for missionary service: _____

_____

God-called missionaries reflect piety and zeal for the Master's kingdom. They have a growing relationship with Jesus Christ, a sound biblical faith, and evidence of disciplined Bible study and prayer. In addition, they maintain a consistent pattern of witness from their concern for the lost. They must share a common commitment to the global task of the IMB that supersedes the provincialism of their specific assignment.

Missionaries who serve with the IMB have always been expected to have personal convictions of truth that are consistent with those held by Southern Baptists. Individual Christians can choose to believe what they will, but those representing Southern Baptists and serving with the IMB are accountable to hold and practice doctrinal convictions consistent with *The Baptist Faith and Message.*

Unlike many mission agencies, we are an entity of our denomination, restricted to sending missionaries from cooperating Southern Baptist churches. Each one approved for appointment must be able to articulate a solid, personal conviction of God's call to overseas service. Accompanying that call is a conviction that God has gifted the candidate for cross-cultural witness and ministry. Those gifts are stirred by training, orientation, equipping, and subsequently living among the people God has selected for them to serve. We would be irresponsible to send into the unsanitary environment and stressful demands of the mission field those who have fragile health, emotional problems, or records of interpersonal conflict. Character and work references are used to assess their levels of maturity and effectiveness and to help discern whether a candidate is prepared to move out of the supportive context of a stateside job to a foreign setting.

The way God calls Christians to mission service is as diverse as the personalities and backgrounds of the missionaries who respond. Many who have felt God's call were nurtured from childhood through mission-education organizations such as Girls in Action and Royal Ambassadors. Today God uses opportunities to participate in short-term volunteer mission trips to call many Christians into full-time missions. Exposed to the lostness of a world without Christ and seeing firsthand how God works through the power of the gospel, volunteers return home with hearts open to God's call. When one businessman came back to the States after a mission trip, he sold his home and business and contacted the IMB. He said, "It is hard to come back home, settle into my comfort zone, enjoy the affluence of an American lifestyle, and continue to pursue wealth and the American dream when I have seen a world dying without Christ and know I could do something about it."

What has God called you to do something about in this lost and dying world? If you are not sure, pause now and pray. Ask Him to show you His plan for your involvement in taking the gospel to the world.

DAY 2
HERE IS MY LIFE: LONG-TERM SERVICE

CAREER MISSIONARIES

Career missionaries are the IMB's primary channel of mission service, with 75 percent of the missionary force appointed for open-ended, long-term assignments. Intending to spend their lives on the mission field, they learn the language and the cultural worldview, nurture relationships, and engage in long-range strategies for evangelizing the people. Their strategic role includes planting and nurturing church growth, discipling and training leaders, and modeling ministries for the indigenous churches of the future. As a result, career missionaries have stringent educational qualifications and requirements for experience prior to appointment.

What proportion of IMB missionaries are career personnel? _____

Why is this the highest-priority category of service? _____

_____

The Missionary Force, 1995–2004

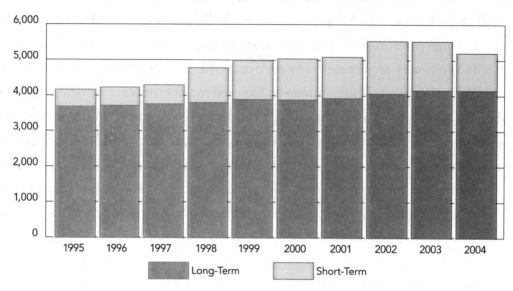

Generally, career missionaries serve until retirement. Family and health needs or a sense of God's leadership to pursue a new direction of ministry may cause missionaries to resign. The average tenure for those who serve until retirement is 23 years, though many serve 30 to 40 years and longer. Recently, two missionaries retired after more than 50 years of active service!

A common misperception is that missionaries who resign are those who have difficulty making adjustments on the mission field. Although some leave the field during their first term, the average tenure of those resigning is more than nine years. At this point they are well into their third term of service and have usually been effective. Perhaps aging parents at home need them as caregivers, or missionary families struggle with children going away to boarding school or college. Research data indicate that 70 percent of missionaries would have chosen not to leave the field, but unavoidable needs and circumstances necessitated that decision.

Look at the graph on this page. List three factors you think contributed to the growth in missionary personnel over the past 10 years.

1. _____

2. _____

3. _____

OTHER MISSIONARIES

Long-term missionaries work alongside missionary associates who may not qualify for career appointment due to age or lack of education. However, associates have extensive professional and church-related ministry experience and are qualified to meet a personnel need that would otherwise go unfilled or would divert other missionaries from their primary assignment. Associates are approved for a four-year term, but the assignment can be renewed, and many missionary associates later fulfill requirements for transferring to career status.

Conversely, the apprentice program was designed for those with adequate education and a confirmed calling but who lacked the professional and ministry experience to qualify for appointment. Getting that experience on the mission field under the tutelage of veteran missionaries was felt to be more valuable than work experience in a stateside setting.

Recently, the IMB began appointing all career missionaries and missionary associates to an initial three- or four-year term as missionary apprentices. They are mentored and trained on the field. This initial term of service confirms their call to overseas ministry and equips them to assume a significant strategic role following a successful evaluation of their term. Others who sense that their ministry should be based in the States can successfully return after completing their three-year commitment without having to resign from missionary service.

DEFINING THE WORD *MISSIONARY*

Considerable controversy surrounds the discussion of what a missionary is. More diverse roles for missionaries create confusion in the minds of some. Many cannot be identified as missionaries because of serving in restricted countries that prohibit a Christian witness. Some still see missionaries as misfits, out of style and out of touch with the real world. On the contrary, missionaries are attractive, gifted, and engaging individuals, obedient to a God-induced passion for reaching a lost world. They forego most amenities and attractions valued by our society.

Because our task is evangelistic, some perceive missionaries only as preachers. Although a preacher's objective is bringing a lost world to saving faith in Jesus Christ, parts of the world prohibit public proclamation by foreigners. An in-your-face confrontational witness is seldom effective, even in our country. Instead, missionaries live their witness and find culturally appropriate ways to disseminate the gospel through many diverse assignments and gifts.

For most of our history Southern Baptists sent missionaries to serve only where missionaries were allowed and welcomed. We became well acquainted with places such as Spain, Brazil, Nigeria, the Philippines, and more than one hundred countries where our missionaries served openly. But in recent years God has been pushing back the barriers that locked multitudes in spiritual darkness. He is opening innovative channels through which missionaries can gain access to restricted countries and can have an impact on unreached people groups with an incarnational witness.

Where are the missionaries? The IMB does not arbitrarily assign personnel to places and jobs irrespective of their personal sense of call and God's leadership. Never could we say that we don't need any other missionaries somewhere in the world. But we encourage missionary candidates to consider going to places of high strategic priority or where the need is most urgent. If our task is to reach all peoples, we cannot send all of our missionaries to only one part of the world. Placement is a matter of prayer, proportion, and priority.

> Check the factors that determine a missionary's assignment. Assess your accuracy by rereading the two preceding paragraphs.
> ❑ The IMB has identified the assignment as a strategic priority.
> ❑ Personnel have been requested by the missionary team on the field.
> ❑ The individual or family has a conviction of God's call and leadership.
> ❑ The individual or family already speaks the language.
> ❑ God has given a candidate a vision and passion for evangelizing a particular people group that is lost.
> ❑ The needs of the assignment match the candidate's unique gifts and experience.

DAY 3
OPPORTUNITIES FOR SHORT-TERM SERVICE

In order to fill the strategic personnel needs overseas and to accommodate the diversity of those who are being called to missionary service, the IMB provides categories of service in addition to career, associate, and apprentice missionaries.

SHORT-TERM SERVICE

One of these avenues of service attracts young adults. Today more and more young adults have developed a passion for missions by participating in volunteer projects during their teens and college years. Many of them relate to the increasingly youthful global population in countries where young people are interested in meeting Americans and learning English.

In 1965 the IMB began a two-year *Journeyman Program* for recent college graduates. This short-term missionary service for single young adults under 30 years of age has proved to be popular over the years and has continued to grow. Volunteers in the Journeyman Program are assigned to universities, community ministries, sports evangelism, and many other channels for sharing the gospel with their generation. Some use degrees in teaching or business to assist in teaching missionary kids or in helping provide logistical support for missionary teams. Others work alongside colleagues in evangelism, discipleship, and church planting.

The appeal of the Journeyman Program began to expand as other adults who were not qualified for career appointment expressed interest in short-term opportunities. Many felt that God was calling them to use their maturity and experience in roles that could benefit the total mission effort and could free long-term personnel for more strategic assignments.

International Service Corps provides a channel of service to other qualified, God-called individuals and couples to serve in two- or three-year short-term assignments. Hundreds of Southern Baptists have taken advantage of this opportunity for mission service. Many return for long-term appointment after having fulfilled the qualifications, convicted of God's call to give their lives to reach a lost world. In fact, over the past two years 43 percent of the career missionaries being appointed had served short-term assignments as journeymen or as International Service Corps missionaries.

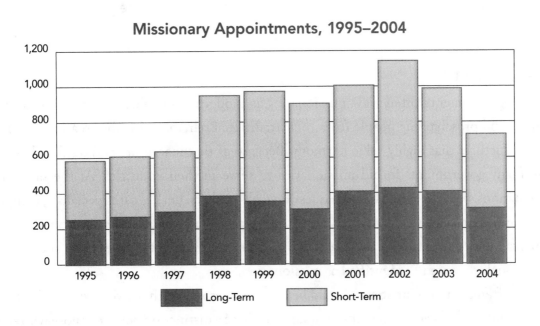

Missionary Appointments, 1995–2004

A more recent phenomenon is the interest being expressed by senior adults in mission service. Older Southern Baptists want to be personally engaged in international missions. Some express a lifelong call that was never fulfilled, but now in their retirement years they would like to serve. If they are in good health, many spiritually mature senior adults desire to devote their final years to a significant ministry. Others are being led to change careers later in life, and God has laid a call to missions on their hearts. A common theme runs through the testimonies of short-term missionaries. As they participated in more and more volunteer trips, the joy and fulfillment of their ministry and witness overseas grew, while the appeal of returning to the comforts of home and a routine job diminished.

Other mission organizations have seized on this trend to launch the Finishers Project, a channel through which retired people can finish life's productive years in missions. When a greater number of mature Southern Baptists applied to the International Service Corps, the *Masters Program* was created for those 50 and older to serve for two or three years.

These older short-term missionaries are bringing needed maturity and years of professional experience to the field. When linked with the passion, energy, and vision of younger missionary families, these seniors are strengthening our missionary teams and effectiveness. Retirement means more than spending time sitting in a rocking chair, playing golf, or fishing when a lost world is waiting to be won!

Match each category of missionary service with its description.

___ 1. Journeymen   a. Young adults serve for two years.

___ 2. International Service Corps   b. Those age 50 and older serve for two or three years.

___ 3. Masters Program   c. Not age-based

OUR MANDATE

Foreign governments often view missionaries as modern colonialists, intent on destroying cultures and proselytizing people from their traditional religions, thereby creating conflict in social structures that highly value harmony. Because of that inaccurate and outdated perception, many governments forbid missionaries to serve in their countries. At the same time, these nations seek Western aid and request English teachers, health-care specialists, computer programmers, business consultants, and others to accelerate their modernization and development. Missionaries can fill these requests in order to become witnesses in an alien culture, even though they are not identified as missionaries.

We often say that Christians should be missionaries where they live. We are all called to witness and to obey the Great Commission. So is there a distinction between those who stay at home and those who plant their lives cross-culturally in foreign lands as teachers and doctors, for example? While we are all to be witnesses, missionaries are called to a special role, just as Abraham was called to leave his home and family as an instrument for God so that all nations would be blessed. Paul expressed a special divine calling to take the gospel to the Gentiles and the regions beyond where the gospel was known.

God has never altered His purpose to evangelize a lost world. He has not withdrawn His mandate to disciple the nations. His promise that the gospel will eventually be proclaimed among every nation, people, tribe, and language still holds. Our response in going to the ends of the earth is not qualified by the missionary label, nor are we limited only to places where foreign governments welcome traditional missionary personnel.

Every church and all of God's people have an obligation to make the gospel known to all people by whatever means and channel God provides. The label is not the issue. Being confined to a narrow, traditional concept is not the point. The source of support and the sending agency are irrelevant. Missionaries respond to our Lord's mandate to use their gifts, skills, and experiences to share the claims of Christ wherever presence can be legitimately gained, even in a hostile world where missionaries are not welcome.

> As you read the following two paragraphs, underline the IMB's four phases of preparation for going overseas.

In order to train and equip missionaries who go overseas, the IMB provides four phases of preparation. The first phase is *to mentor candidates in the experience and training* that will prepare them for missionary service prior to their being approved for appointment. Following appointment, they *participate in a seven-week field-preparation orientation* at the Missionary Learning Center near IMB headquarters in Richmond, Virginia. This facility can accommodate several hundred missionaries and their families. The Learning Center is also used for candidate conferences, stateside-assignment conferences for veteran missionaries rotating in from the field, and other training events.

A third on-the-field phase of training and orientation occurs throughout the apprentice term or the entire short-term assignment when personnel arrive overseas. The greatest emphasis is placed on *learning the language and adjusting to the culture*. The final phase is an ongoing program of *life development and continuing education* provided by the IMB's International Centre for Excellence in Leadership through self-study courses and modules.

Each of the four phases for training missionary personnel focuses on seven dimensions that form the core of missionary competencies:

1. Discipleship and spiritual growth
2. Servant leadership
3. Cross-cultural witness
4. Family strength and nurture
5. Missions mobilization
6. Facilitating church-planting movements
7. Being a team player

Four Phases of Orientation and
Seven Dimensions of Field-Personnel Competencies

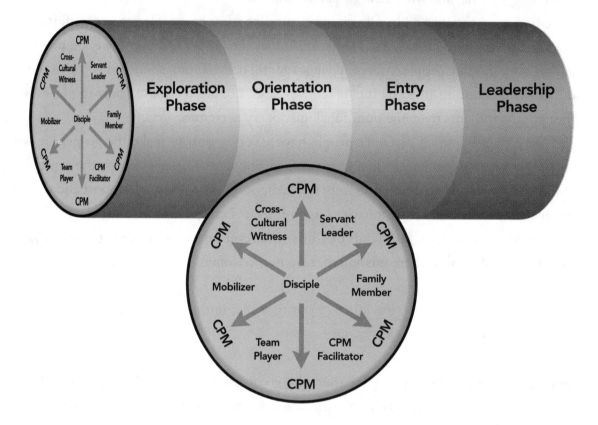

Study the seven competencies printed on the wheel on this page. According to your opinion, number them in priority order on the wheel.

DAY 4
SENDERS AND MOBILIZERS

The IMB serves as the sending agency for more than 43,000 local Southern Baptist churches from which missionaries are called. The churches are a channel through which missionaries can be equipped and supported while working together in a structure of mutual accountability. Sadly, many churches have never had a missionary from their congregations called to serve overseas. For others it has been many years, perhaps even generations, since they had members express a call to overseas missions.

Certainly, the primary factor in those who are called is God's sovereignty. But when so few are hearing that call relative to the needs of a lost world, indicators reveal a neglected emphasis. A lack of passion for missions and a deficiency in our preaching and teaching could be reasons Christians are not stirred to offer themselves for missionary service. Once a decision to surrender for missions is made, the local church should continue to have a sense of ownership in sending out their missionaries. Sending missionaries is a biblical calling of the church, not of a denominational agency.

What role should the local church have in sending missionaries?

_____

_____

THE COOPERATIVE PROGRAM

When money is allocated to the Cooperative Program and additional gifts are given to the Lottie Moon Christmas Offering® for International Missions, the funds should be seen as personal support for the church's missionary as well as for thousands of other missionaries. Churches that do not have missionaries from their congregations are encouraged to adopt missionaries. By staying informed, connected, and involved, they can have a biblical sense of ownership for sending and supporting missionaries. The IMB exists to assist and serve the churches in this task.

Throughout the history of the Southern Baptist Convention (SBC), some have challenged the cooperative principles that enable autonomous churches to work together in missions, evangelism, education, and ministry. Often the only thing that distinguishes many independent and Bible Baptist churches from the SBC is their unwillingness to work in cooperation with one another. Those outside the SBC often view the Convention, with its boards and agencies, as a denominational hierarchy that exists to control and manage the churches' work. In fact, local churches create and empower the entities and agencies of the denomination to serve and facilitate the churches to accomplish more together than they could do individually.

In the 19th century T. P. Crawford, a missionary to China, concluded that sending missionaries through the Foreign Mission Board (as the IMB was known then) was unbiblical. He led most of the North China Mission to secede from the Foreign Mission Board. They eventually returned when the challenge of raising independent support infringed on their missionary work and required a parallel organization in the United States to be formed to raise their support and channel it to the field. Today splinter organizations, based on the premise that churches should appoint and send their own missionaries, actually replicate the work of the IMB in providing services to churches such as mobilization and enlistment, orientation and training, the coordination of travel and financial services, and the direction of field strategies.

> Name three ways the IMB serves Southern Baptist churches by sending missionaries.
>
> 1. _____
>
> 2. _____
>
> 3. _____

Many Southern Baptist churches support missionaries who serve with other organizations. But most provide only a portion or token support to personnel who are sent out independently. Many of our largest churches could provide full support for one or more families overseas, but most could not. Most Southern Baptist churches find it difficult to provide support beyond the needs of their own staff and local expenses. However, when churches cooperatively join together to provide financial support, we can send many more missionaries. Missionary families don't have to enlist support directly. Rather than spending time finding churches to support them—or delaying going to the field until they can find that support—the Cooperative Program supplies it. Cooperation is biblical, and it empowers kingdom growth!

A church could decide to raise the salary and support of a missionary family and send them out directly. But where would they find adequate orientation and training with a community of others who are going to the field? The IMB provides the orientation and training of newly commissioned missionaries at the IMB's Missionary Learning Center.

Independent missionaries lack logistical support because churches usually fail to calculate the cost of travel expenses, the shipment of freight, provisions for children's education, medical expenses, insurance to cover major catastrophes, possible medical evacuation, disability, and an adequate pension program. The independent missionary is on his own when obtaining a visa or arranging for housing and transportation on the field. Having a global organization like the IMB to provide these services benefits the churches from which missionaries are called.

The grass withered in the hot sun. Waterholes and riverbeds were dry and cracked. Animals died from starvation and thirst. People would be next. In desperation villagers dug deep holes in the riverbeds in search of water. Everyone knew that rain was needed, but it was not the rainy season.

Villagers decided to conduct a rain dance to plead with the rain god and the ancestors to send rain. One new believer in Jesus consulted the missionary who lived in their village. "Pastor, what should we do?" she asked. "Some people want to pray to the rain god."

"Let's review some of the characteristics of God," the missionary suggested. "The true God controls all things. God is all-powerful and omniscient. He knows we need rain. I believe God is waiting for us to ask Him. Let's put our faith in God and pray to Him. Let's ask God for rain."

That night the small group of believers earnestly prayed for rain. Before the witch doctors could arrange a proper rain dance, the rains came out of season and continued for a week! The young woman later testified, "I told my father that the pastor led us in prayer for rain. When it rained, my father said he could see that Jesus had great power. I explained to him that God is the most powerful of all!"

Many people need to know the omnipotent God, who can bring them out of darkness and fear to a life filled with the Living Water.

—FAYE; CENTRAL, EASTERN, AND SOUTHERN AFRICA

Check the actions that are valid reasons for the IMB to serve churches by sending and supporting God-called missionaries.

❑ 1. Provides adequate support on the field
❑ 2. Validates a candidate's qualifications and call
❑ 3. Disburses support around the world
❑ 4. Replaces the church's responsibility in sending missionaries
❑ 5. Provides adequate training and preparation
❑ 6. Builds a community of support and accountability
❑ 7. Takes care of travel, children's education, and health-care needs
❑ 8. Alleviates any responsibility for personal contact with missionaries
❑ 9. Discourages involvement in the missionary's work

DAY 5
NURTURING A MISSIONS LIFESTYLE

Recently, the testimonies of two missionaries crossed my desk. One is a strategy coordinator focusing on a people group that has never had access to the gospel. The other is a strategy coordinator seeking to reach lost population segments in a country where missionaries have served for more than one hundred years. Both are driven by a passion to provide the people to whom they are called an opportunity to know Jesus.

One had gone to a place in the Last Frontier where evangelism is prohibited and to people who have been deprived of the gospel. He bemoaned the fact that "many peoples have remained locked in spiritual bondage to their animistic practices for all of history because our traditional approach has been to go only where we were invited." He continued: "The goal of world evangelization is about getting at lostness! It requires more folks who are ready to die ... in order to go into areas where the gospel hasn't yet penetrated. We must be willing to risk failure but keep pushing the limits of our ability to go to the edge and mobilize others to do the same. We hear a lot about Muslim extremists, but where are the Christian extremists who have the vision, passion, and drive to go to the hard places?"

The other missionary expressed gratitude for those who had preceded him when the country where he now serves was a difficult frontier field. In answer to the question of why God led him to a country where missionaries were welcome and the harvest had been plentiful, he said it was because of a "passion and zeal for the tens of millions who remain unevangelized. Even though I serve on a traditional and open field, few of us live in sheltered environments, protected from harm or persecution. We have gone out with national co-workers to share the gospel and have been threatened, attacked, stoned, and assaulted. I would be willing to lay down my life for the sake of the lost people we are trying to reach. Is the value of a soul in an unreached people group any greater than one who has had access to the gospel but has never heard and understood it? The eternity in hell that awaits all without Christ is the same!"

A PASSION TO SHARE JESUS

These two missionaries said much more. Their words expressed their vision and their strategy for seeing the Great Commission fulfilled on their fields of service. Missionary personnel have a strong sense of call and a passion for their places of service. Why would someone go to a place uninvited or live where their Christian witness is not welcome? Why does one embrace hardship and danger, subjecting his family to isolation and uncertainty?

The answer is the same reason anyone responds to God's call—a passion to reach the lost with the good news of Jesus Christ. The passion that drives any missionary, whether on a traditional field or the Last Frontier, is the same. This passion flows from God's heart for a lost and dying world. Those whom God calls are those who are driven to do whatever it takes to see the walls of lostness breached for the sake of the kingdom of God.

These are the ones who say with Isaiah, "Here I am. Send me" (Isa. 6:8) in response to God's plea for someone to go into the darkness. We must eradicate the darkness by shining the light of the gospel among all peoples of the world. I've heard pathos in the plea that goes out from missionaries all over the world to mobilize workers, church partners, and intercessors. They are asking God for individuals or a church family who will share their burden and plead with the Lord of the harvest until the strongholds are destroyed and the kingdom of God has come to the ends of the earth.

> Describe what drives a missionary's passion, whether serving among an unreached people group or where churches have been planted.

_____

_____

A MISSIONS LIFESTYLE

We are grateful for Southern Baptists' faithfulness in giving to missions through the Cooperative Program and the Lottie Moon Christmas Offering® for International Missions, all of which is fully utilized in our budget of ministry and missionary support. However, the potential of continuing kingdom growth until the Great Commission has been completed is enhanced by those who invest in future mission efforts. I'm excited to think about being among that great cloud of witnesses watching the resources and material wealth with which God has blessed us continue to be used to reach a lost world. To accomplish that vision, we must cultivate a missions lifestyle, even here at home.

God has blessed many in our churches with profitable investments and significant wealth. As they move into the later years of life, they think about the transfer of their assets. Are these decisions based on a kingdom perspective? Often the IMB receives notification from a family or a state Baptist foundation that a trust or portion of someone's estate has been allocated to the IMB. Many dedicated Southern Baptists have become aware that their wealth can live beyond their own witness and influence here on earth to continue to extend the kingdom of God. Unless otherwise designated by the donor, gifts from these wills and trusts go into an endowment to ensure the future of mission efforts to share the gospel around the world. Instead of being exhausted as a gift to a one-time need, these funds continue to multiply far beyond the initial investment to provide resources for global missions indefinitely.

Many will not live to see the day when the final people group is reached. But they can have a part in completing the task by setting up trusts, including the IMB in their wills, and providing kingdom resources that will outlive them. We cannot take our wealth with us, but it can continue to reap eternal dividends long after we have gone on to fellowship with our Lord Jesus Christ in heaven!

Is the following statement true or false? Only missionaries are called to a missions lifestyle. Circle one: True   False

Write ways a stateside church member can reflect a missions lifestyle. Name at least one action in four of the following areas.

Awareness of lostness: _____

Praying: _____

Personal stewardship: _____

Witnessing: _____

Missions advocacy: _____

Mobilization: _____

Financial investments: _____

Openness to God's call: _____

1. "Husband and Wife Imparting Faith in Heavily Muslim City in Africa," Baptist Press [online], 12 December 2005 [cited 9 January 2006]. Available from the Internet: *www.bpnews.net*. Names changed for security reasons.

Week 7
MAKING A GLOBAL IMPACT

VERSES TO REMEMBER

"All the ends of the earth will remember
and turn to the LORD.
All the families of the nations
will bow down before You,
for kingship belongs to the LORD;
He rules over the nations."

PSALM 22:27-28

Located on the northwest side of urban Houston, a 230-member church is made up of retirees, young couples with small children, and a few singles. "We're not a wealthy church," said the pastor, but their mission offerings have grown from $2,000 to $40,000—not a small task. "I believe the difference has been living the experience," the pastor continued. "Missions is our passion, our purpose. It's not what we do between Christmas parties."

In 2005 the church sent members on volunteer mission trips to the Arabian Peninsula, Indonesia, Bangladesh, Mexico, and northeast Africa. Amazingly, the expenses haven't gotten in the way of the church's budget. "As the people come and the projects come, the money comes," the pastor said. "God honors churches that make missions a priority."[1]

How would you define the word *worldview?* Do you know the differences between the worldviews of Hindus and Buddhists? How would those beliefs affect a missionary's strategy in reaching these lost people groups? Understanding cross-cultural worldviews helps short-term volunteer groups as well as churches that connect with a specific missionary or adopt a people group. This week you will continue to focus on new strategies used by the International Mission Board and ways you and your church can be a part of those strategies.

DAY 1
SHORT-TERM VOLUNTEER INVOLVEMENT

Although record numbers of missionaries are being sent, Southern Baptists still have only one missionary unit—a family or single person—for every 1.6 million people in the world. We would have to double the number of missionaries just to have one person assigned to every unreached people group, some of which number in the millions. We will likely fail to fulfill the Great Commission if we rely only on full-time missionaries. Thousands of volunteers joining in the effort enhance the potential of our witness around the world.

> How would you encourage the 43,000 Southern Baptist churches to send even one volunteer team overseas each year? What do you think the impact would be?
>
> _____
>
> _____
>
> _____

VOLUNTEERS ON THE FIELD

My first experience with short-term volunteers came during my temporary assignment to India years ago. Frequently, medical volunteers came to a hospital, contributing their services and training staff. In the evenings they often went to the village churches and found abundant opportunities for an evangelistic witness. Giving encouragement to the lay pastors was another gratifying experience. Two years into the emerging church-growth movement, an American physician suggested bringing a group of volunteers to concentrate on evangelistic outreach. We readily agreed that the climate was good for such a project. When he asked how many to enlist, we replied, "As many as you can get to come," expecting a group of 12 to 15 people. We were startled to receive news that 55 Americans would come.

After the planeload of Americans disembarked in Bangalore and had a day of rest and orientation, the plan was to disperse the volunteers in pairs with a national counterpart and a translator. They would saturate a neighborhood or a village with door-to-door witnessing. Some would share their testimonies in public places. The day would culminate in an evening evangelistic service at a church or in the home of a sympathetic Christian or inquirer.

Most of the Southern Baptist volunteers, from teenagers to senior adults, had never been overseas before. The 30 hours of travel, including hours in transit lounges in Amsterdam and Delhi, abruptly challenged their southern provincialism. Several took the train to Madras, and another group flew to Bombay to share the blessings of ministry with fledgling churches. Each day's briefing included reminders about cultural sensitivities and an absolute prohibition against eating any food on the streets or in homes. Volunteers left the hotel with bottles of water, crackers, and candy bars to sustain them until their return for a late dinner in the evening. Miraculously, only six succumbed to "Delhi belly" after drinking the sweet, syrupy tea offered as a gesture of hospitality in each home.

However, panic broke out when each pair of volunteers was told to decide which one would preach each night. Only six pastors had arrived with the American group. One man, a telephone lineman, expressed the feelings of others by saying he had never preached, didn't have any sermons, and didn't know how to get them! Not until they gathered in the little house groups did the image of an American pulpit vanish, and they recognized the validity of telling a Bible story about Jesus and sharing the plan of salvation. Each volunteer had written a personal testimony, which had then been translated and reproduced on paper with the translation on one side and English on the other. As the volunteers shared their experience in English, the translators read the testimony in the heart language of the people.

The team left gospel tracts with those who listened or spoke to them. The first night the telephone lineman excitedly entered the hotel reporting that in the worship service he led, 10 persons had prayed to receive Christ. At the end of the week more than two thousand professions of faith were recorded, all in the context of neighborhoods where follow-up could be done. Potential churches were started in 18 locations.

Number the following characteristics of a mission volunteer in order of importance, with 1 being most important and 5 being least important.

___ Use a good translator

___ Reflect love for the people

___ Have financial resources to travel

___ Preach effective sermons

___ Feel burdened for the lostness of a people group

THE IMPACT OF SHORT-TERM VOLUNTEERS

Missionaries realized years ago that their witness could be vastly multiplied by teams of short-term volunteers. An obvious need was giving attention to all of the local Baptist churches on the mission field. A program linking stateside churches with those overseas proved to encourage and bless both. In addition, volunteer teams came for evangelistic emphases. Paired with local church members, they witnessed in the community and led training on stewardship, discipleship, and many other ministries.

Many state conventions assumed the coordination of prolonged state-to-national partnerships by enlisting volunteers and providing orientation. The numbers of volunteers escalated to more than 30,000 in 2004. Although volunteer teams include many pastors and church-staff members, they are primarily lay men and women who take vacation time and raise their own support for travel and expenses to share the gospel and meet needs on the mission field.

Check the skills that are essential to the effectiveness of short-term volunteers.

❑ 1. Ability to speak the local language

❑ 2. Advanced-education degree or professional skill

❑ 3. Seminary training or church-staff experience

❑ 4. Personal testimony of having been born again

❑ 5. Desire for lost people to know Jesus

❑ 6. Willingness to live without comforts and conveniences

❑ 7. Extensive travel experience

Volunteer mission teams leave an impact on the fields where they minister. Projects vary from doing research and participating in prayerwalks to training lay pastors. When a natural disaster strikes, Southern Baptist volunteers can respond effectively anywhere in the world. State disaster-relief coordinators can mobilize volunteer teams at a moment's notice. Choirs, athletic teams, medical teams, and a variety of other special projects provide channels for anyone to share a witness overseas. Tolerating jet lag and eating strange foods are worth the opportunity to share Christ with people who would not otherwise hear. God is demonstrating His power all over the world, and His people are saying, "I'm available. I'll go and do what I can." And the kingdom continues to grow.

> How often should a person consider participating in a volunteer mission trip?
> ❏ At least once in a lifetime
> ❏ Once a year
> ❏ When he or she can afford it
> ❏ As often as God leads

DAY 2
SERVING CONSISTENTLY WITH FIELD STRATEGIES

Missionaries do not work alone. They join a team in a coordinated strategy to make an impact on unreached people groups and to evangelize their assigned countries and population segments. They do not go as Lone Rangers to do their thing, oblivious to the callings of colleagues and national partners. Missionaries are expected to be accountable to one another and to the Southern Baptist churches that send them and support them. They are to fulfill their assignments with mutual respect and in cooperation with others as a team that testifies to a common passion for the task. The unity of the Spirit that calls and indwells each missionary provides a synergy that enables a greater kingdom impact than the sum efforts of many individuals. The cooperation, accountability, and mutual respect that are expected of missionaries on the field reflect basic biblical standards for the way the body of Christ is to function.

SOWING FOR A GREATER HARVEST

Previously, Southern Baptist field missionaries belonged to large, nationwide organizations that determined the strategies and budgets for everyone working within a specific country. They are now organized into local teams that focus on specific people groups, cities, and population segments. They require a small number of logistical support teams to assist in financial services and managing property and travel. Each one is accountable to one another rather than to a hierarchy of administrators.

This team structure has decentralized strategic planning to give ownership of strategies to those who actually carry out the work, relate to national partners, and are immersed in the task. Regional leadership teams seek to provide the resources needed and keep the strategy focused on the vision of reaching people through church-planting movements.

A continuing missiological tension exists between deploying personnel to unreached people groups in the Last Frontier and continuing to send missionaries to traditional, historical fields where the harvest is considered to be ripe. Does concentrating resources on the massive unreached population of China and south Asia, where there are more unreached people groups yet to be engaged than in all the rest of the world, imply that responsive fields with ripe harvests are being neglected? Are we wasting personnel and resources in establishing platforms and ministries of sowing in the Muslim world, where there is meager response, instead of going to open fields where greater evangelistic results can be realized? The answer must be considered from theological, missiological, and practical perspectives.

Theologically, the gospel is the power of God that leads to salvation. The Spirit of God indwells the message of the gospel to draw all people to Jesus Christ. But response always depends on access. Believing that God desires that all peoples know and worship Him and believing in the power of the gospel, we can only segment the world into current harvest fields and neglected harvest fields.

"We have discovered where we sow abundantly, we reap abundantly; where we sow sparingly, we reap sparingly. The only reason we do not have a more abundant harvest in the Muslim world is we haven't found a way to sow the gospel more abundantly."
—A WORKER IN NORTHERN AFRICA

Missiologically, a missionary's task is to work himself out of a job. We are to proclaim the gospel, win people to Christ, plant churches, train leaders, and move on to the fringes of lostness. A principle characterizes our task: the resources are in the harvest. In other words, winning a lost world is not the exclusive task of Western, cross-cultural missionaries propagating a patronizing dependency on their presence and leadership. The massive numbers of local believers and national churches represent the potential for completing the task. They join the task of winning the lost around them and sending out missionaries to neighboring people groups.

Read Romans 15:19-21. The Apostle Paul said, "I have fully proclaimed the good news about the Messiah from Jerusalem all the way around to Illyricum. So my aim is to evangelize where Christ has not been named ... and those who have not heard will understand."

How did Paul describe the missionary task? _____

Not everyone from Jerusalem to Illyricum had been won or discipled, nor had all people in this area even heard the gospel. But the good news of the gospel had been made accessible to those regions, and churches had been planted to be a nucleus of witness in those locations. Meanwhile, Paul went on to the regions where people did not yet have access to the gospel.

What is a harvest? _____

Theologically, missiologically, and practically, our perception of what a harvest is may actually be distorted by numbers. A large response to the gospel is always contingent on access, which usually includes a long history of witness, multiple churches, and local believers who proclaim the gospel. If there are places where people are not considered responsive, it may simply be because no one has given them an opportunity to hear and understand. As we are told in Romans 10:14, "How can they call on Him in whom they have not believed? And how can they believe without hearing about Him?"

The IMB bases an accurate assessment of harvest and responsiveness on how many new believers come to faith in Christ and are baptized, relative to the number of believers within a geographic entity or people group. The assessment also takes into account how many new churches are started relative to the number of established churches. A newly reached people group may have only 1,000 baptized believers, but over a given period of time they may have reached and baptized 10,000 new believers. Another country that has been evangelized and has 1,000,000 baptized believers may baptize 20,000 new believers. The larger number won to Christ does not indicate a greater responsiveness and harvest.

Choose the option from each pair that indicates greater potential evangelistic response.

❑ 100 existing churches planting 10 new churches
❑ 10 existing churches planting 100 new churches

❑ 2 new churches averaging 200 members each
❑ 10 new churches averaging 30 members each

❑ A country with 1,000 Baptist churches reporting 2,000 baptisms
❑ A country with 50 Baptist churches reporting 1,000 baptisms

If we recognize that the resources are in the harvest and that our global mission task is not the unique and exclusive role of missionaries alone, we gain a perspective on the decision of deploying missionaries and making the gospel accessible to unreached people groups.

What does this expression mean: "The resources are in the harvest"?

_____

_____

We also recognize other available resources:

1. The first resource is *Baptist partners around the world.* Where churches have been planted, grown, matured, and established national conventions, the nationals can assume a large part of the responsibility for the task. Our role, in partnership, is to train and encourage them in a catalytic role.

2. Priorities and needs are also affected by the presence of *other evangelical believers, churches, and mission agencies.* We would be foolish to duplicate efforts in one area while other parts of the world remain neglected.

3. A third resource is the massive numbers of *volunteers* who are mobilized by our own Southern Baptist churches. In places where significant numbers of volunteers can partner with our missionaries and relate to national churches, they no longer depend on missionaries to develop methodologies for evangelism efforts and discipleship training. Often, people-group strategies can be relinquished to stateside church partners and volunteer teams.

Name three potential personnel resources other than IMB missionaries whom God is using to reach a lost world.

1. _____

2. _____

3. _____

DAY 3
UNDERSTANDING CROSS-CULTURAL WORLDVIEWS

Missions is the task of taking the gospel cross-culturally and geographically beyond where we live to give all peoples the opportunity to hear, understand, and respond to the gospel in their own cultural contexts. We can readily understand some of the barriers that keep a lost world from being evangelized, such as geographic and language barriers. However, in every culture subtle barriers exist that are created by the worldview of the people. A worldview is the way someone perceives and relates to the world. Often, many who hear the words and presentation of the gospel do not understand it with the same meaning as the person communicating it.

Missions: *The task of taking the gospel cross-culturally and geographically beyond where we live to give all peoples the opportunity to hear, understand, and respond to the gospel in their own cultural contexts*

Worldview: *The assumptions and beliefs that guide someone's thoughts, attitudes, and actions*

Obviously, when we travel to other countries, people speak other languages. They dress differently and eat different foods. But their worldview is not always readily discernible. Why do they believe what they do? What are their patterns of relationships and behavior?

Why is it important that people hear and understand the gospel in their own cultural contexts?

_____

_____

UNDERSTANDING WORLDVIEWS

Our Western culture is very individualistic; people make their own decisions and attempt to do whatever they want. But inhabitants of other cultures would not think of making a decision apart from the approval and consensus of the group or community. Recently, I traveled throughout west Africa. As a group of us went into villages with our missionaries, it would have been unthinkable to visit any of the people without first approaching the village chief, announcing our arrival as outsiders, and showing proper respect. Not only would the people have refused to receive us, but we would have also created a barrier to communication and relationships by being perceived as arrogant, insensitive, and abrasive foreigners.

We Americans quickly discerned that certain behaviors and protocol must be observed. In many places throughout the world giving or receiving anything with the left hand is considered offensive. In Thailand showing the bottom of one's foot or pointing with the foot is considered an insult, even vulgar. These behaviors are not just a matter of people having strange quirks; people have reasons for all they do, and these reasons are based in cultural worldviews.

In many places people see life as controlled by the spirit world. Therefore, they spend all of their lives, from birth to death, doing things that bring the favor of the spirits or appease them. Not only in Africa but also around the world, amulets, fetishes, good-luck charms, and superstitions prevail. Most cultures believe that the spirits of ancestors linger and constantly interact with living people. Buddhists are diligent to place offerings in spirit houses in the corners of their yards and to do good deeds to accumulate karma or merit. The spirit world determines how people prepare food, kill a chicken, or build a house. These decisions are believed to determine someone's fortunes.

People may hear the words of the gospel, but their meaning is filtered through the perceptions of their own culture. In trying to share John 3:16 with a Buddhist, a witness immediately encounters the barrier of who God is, because Buddhists have no concept of an almighty divine being. When you say that God loved the world so much that He gave His only Son as a sacrifice for our sin, the statement makes no sense at all. Buddhists' only concept of love is an erotic, self-serving love. They cannot comprehend that someone would give to another person because of love. They don't see the world, or cosmos, as having value and as meriting redemption. Rather, they view the world as something to escape by attaining enlightenment through endless reincarnations.

To Buddhists and Hindus the distinction between good and evil, birth and death, growth and decay is only an illusion. They are like the two sides of a coin that is one and inseparable. These beliefs have a lot to do with determining moral concepts—or the lack of them. Because the Hindu worldview includes a pantheon of millions of deities, Hindus find it easy to accept Jesus as Savior and add Him to their litany of gods.

The basic premise of our witness and need to trust Jesus as Savior rests on the fact of humans' sin and separation from God, but many cultural worldviews do not include any responsibility for personal sin. Muslims have a fatalistic view of life in which everything, including their ultimate salvation, is determined by *insha Allah,* or Allah's will, and no one can do anything to change his or her fortune and destiny. Islam is a monotheistic faith, that is, one god above all, who does not represent himself in three persons as does the Christian God. However, when

I visited Muslim countries, I was unprepared for the prevalent belief in the spirit world. For example, offerings of rice and flowers are placed at intersections to ensure safety.

Name at least three cultural traditions that differ from your worldview.

1. _____

2. _____

3. _____

OUR CULTURAL WORLDVIEW

American culture neatly categorizes life into the sacred and the secular, but in most cultures religion is intertwined with all aspects of life. We think individuals overseas can simply choose to become Christians without major life changes. However, in many cultures, becoming a Christian means denying personal citizenship and ethnicity and rejecting society.

Christians are among the few who gather at a specific time for corporate worship. For most of the world, religion is tied to life events and is practiced only because of certain needs that arise. A devotee lights a candle in a Catholic church. A follower of Buddhism chants and shakes the *jos* sticks in a Buddhist temple so that a business will prosper, a sick mother will be healed, a barren wife will get pregnant, or a student will pass his exams. An American observed a Chinese man putting food on the tomb of his recently deceased relative. The American asked when he thought the deceased would eat the food. The Chinese friend replied, "When your deceased relatives smell the flowers you put on their graves." Customs, traditions, and practices relate to our worldview and provide strong filters for perceiving the gospel message.

Check actions you would be willing to take to prepare for an effective cross-cultural witness.
❑ Research and read books and articles about the host culture
❑ Confer with missionaries who serve among the people group
❑ Ask questions of people you meet in other countries to show an interest in understanding them and their way of life
❑ Respect the advice of a national pastor or translator rather than presuming to do things your way
❑ Observe how people act and relate to one another

Americans, who view honesty as a desired value, find it difficult to understand that saving face is much more important for most cultures. Because the highest good is social acceptance, someone would never offend another. If I ordered work to be done and expected it to be finished today, a laborer would tell me that it would be completed even though he knew it would not. It is considered better to lie than to offend and disappoint someone. The same situation occurs when a foreign guest asks someone to make a decision to accept Christ as Savior. Their cultural worldview would make it unacceptable to offend an honored guest by failing to respond as requested.

Can the gospel overcome cultural barriers and penetrate contradictory worldviews? Of course it can, but the one who seeks to communicate a concept of God and His love must be sensitive to other worldviews, understand how concepts are being perceived, and share the gospel in a way that it can be received.

Identify the following statements as true (T) or false (F).
_____ 1. People's daily behavior has little to do with their religious convictions.
_____ 2. Americans tend to be egocentric in thinking our way is right or superior to others.
_____ 3. People in other cultures have strange traditions and practices because they are uneducated and don't know any better.
_____ 4. Often a new believer feels that he has to deny his cultural identity in order to become a Christian.
_____ 5. The truth of the gospel has the power to transcend cultural differences.

DAY 4
CHURCHES OWNING THE TASK

Churches are becoming increasingly interested in direct, ongoing involvement in mission strategies through occasional participation in short-term mission trips. They are beginning to recognize that God did not call them just to reach their cities and local communities. Each church can have a role in advancing kingdom growth and fulfilling the Great Commission to the ends of the earth.

The IMB supports this paradigm shift to partnerships and personal relationships by providing opportunities for churches to be directly involved in overseas mission strategies and to own responsibility for reaching specific population segments for Christ. Through years of volunteer involvement, many churches have developed their own independent mission programs in various parts of the world. They have built relationships with national Baptist leaders and have discovered they did not need the IMB to provide contacts, arrange projects, and help make travel arrangements.

THE VANISHING MIDDLEMAN

A characteristic of contemporary society is that people and organizations, including churches, are no longer interested in having a middleman serve as a mediator between them and the action. They are not interested in having to jump through bureaucratic hoops in order to do missions. Churches are willing to cooperate with others but want a face on missions. They are willing to give generously but also want to be involved with what they are giving to support. They want personal relationships with their missionaries.

Rather than seeing this trend as infringing on the IMB's programs and strategies, we consider it an asset that radically multiplies the potential for kingdom growth.

> Why is it important for a church to confer with missionaries on the field
> to determine the church's mission strategies and ministries?

Missionaries are encouraged to take initiative in asking churches to connect with them as their personal missionaries. These may be churches where they grew up and were members, where they served on the staff, where their families are members, or where God has brought about a relationship. Although the church's gifts and offerings to the Cooperative Program and the Lottie Moon Christmas Offering® for International Missions help support more than five thousand international missionaries, these churches have personalized the channels of support. They know their gifts help meet the needs of their missionary as well as the needs of others, and they understand what those needs are.

A MISSIONARY CONNECTION

Churches are connecting with other missionaries who have been in their churches on a state-side assignment or who relate to the church's involvement overseas. The missionaries are accountable to communicate and report to these churches so that churches can stay abreast of what God is doing in distant lands. This personal relationship makes the church's prayer ministry more relevant as members respond to specific needs.

Name the missionaries with whom you are acquainted and where they serve.

_____

_____

One missionary organized a personal team of 15 to 20 people to serve as a supportive liaison between his family and the church he had left. The team was charged with maintaining contact and ministering to the needs of the missionary's family. One person nurtured a prayer network. Another ministered to the missionary's children by occasionally sending toys and gifts. Others checked on the missionary's aging parents and arranged for a power of attorney. The team assisted in storing belongings left behind and offered help if something had to be purchased and shipped from the States. Instead of praying for God to bless a nameless and faceless missionary, church members felt personally involved in their support and felt pride in sharing the results of the missionary's ministry.

ADOPT A PEOPLE GROUP

Many churches begin personal involvement in kingdom growth by adopting people groups in a PRAYERPlus Partnership—praying for the people plus a commitment to do whatever God leads them to do. Other churches are moving beyond a partnership with missionaries to accept the challenge of adopting an unreached people group where no missionary is available to be assigned. At this point the IMB is giving priority in its global strategies to reaching people groups with populations of one hundred thousand or more. But most of the still unreached people groups are micro-peoples with populations far fewer than that. Generally, they are located in remote districts that are untouched by the gospel.

The South America region launched a strategy called REAP—Rapid Entry Advance Plan. They train churches how to access the sparsely populated indigenous tribes scattered throughout mountain valleys of the Andes with no gospel witness in their heart languages. With the assistance of national Christians who are bilingual, these churches actually function as the strategy coordinator for a people group where no missionaries are assigned.

An identical situation exists in west Africa, where most of the 1,400 tribal and people groups have populations of fewer than 15,000. Although we will never have enough missionaries to focus on reaching each one, we hope that efforts to reach the major people groups will enable them to spread the gospel to the smaller ones. But the process of evangelizing the peoples of west Africa could be vastly accelerated if churches assumed responsibility for adopting people groups who have no one working among them. At least the churches could intercede for them before God's throne. Most likely, God would lead them to do more than pray.

As missionaries concentrate on pushing to the edge of lostness, stateside church partners can come alongside them to relate to the established churches overseas, encouraging pastors, discipling new believers, and working with the members in evangelistic outreach to plant new churches. Often, the expansion of missionary efforts to unevangelized areas is delayed by the need to nurture established work. A partner church that assists with this need can liberate missionaries to focus on the main task of missions, for which they are called and equipped.

What are some ways your church could encourage and support specific missionaries and/or people groups?

_____

_____

DAY 5
SUSTAINING CONTINUING PARTNERSHIPS

Churches are discovering a new passion for ministry and are seeing an unprecedented involvement of their members in missions. As they embrace God's heart for the world, their churches are transformed into worldwide mission centers. In one church the pastor began to recognize that the purpose of worship and Bible study is to equip his people to witness and minister in the world. He said to his congregation, "We are no longer going to call our sanctuary our worship center. It is our global outreach center. God said in Psalm 46:10,

> *'Stop ... and know that I am God,*
> *exalted among the nations, exalted on the earth.'*

The reason we gather to worship is to know God deeper and be equipped to exalt Him throughout the world."

EMPOWERING KINGDOM GROWTH

Before ascending to heaven after His crucifixion and resurrection, Jesus issued this challenge to His followers: "'You will receive power when the Holy Spirit has come upon you, and you will be My witnesses in Jerusalem, in all Judea and Samaria, and to the ends of the earth'" (Acts 1:8). A church that embraces the Acts 1:8 Challenge must be intentional about engaging the total task of God's mission. It must awaken its members to God's calling and must cooperate with others to take the gospel to all peoples. It must be consciously committed to being involved in its community (Jerusalem), in its state (Judea), throughout the North American continent (Samaria), and throughout the world (ends of the earth).

> **Acts 1:8 Challenge:** *A call for Southern Baptist churches to cooperate with their local Baptist association, their state convention, the North American Mission Board, and the International Mission Board to take the gospel to their community (Jerusalem), region (Judea), continent (Samaria), and the world (ends of the earth)*

The level of involvement a church reaches in international missions is usually multiplied many times over by its renewed commitment to mission work in North America, its own state, and its community. Due to the lower cost and convenience of mobilizing people for ministries nearer home, churches that catch a vision for global missions are usually those that are most actively involved in their associations, in their state conventions, and in partnerships with the North American Mission Board.

> Is your church an Acts 1:8 church?   ❏ Yes   ❏ No

When the Southern Baptist Convention adopted the vision of Empowering Kingdom Growth, it recognized that all we do should result in the expansion and growth of God's kingdom. The denomination's work at every level is to serve and enable local churches to carry out that purpose. Churches do not support the denomination so that it can carry on kingdom work on their behalf; the denomination and its entities exist to support and facilitate local churches to be more effective in fulfilling their kingdom task.

Churches are awakening to the fact that God has commanded His church to be on mission to the ends of the earth. This command does not diminish the role and importance of missionaries. In fact, local churches fulfill their mission task most effectively when they are connected with personnel on the field. This task can be successful only through a commitment to an ongoing partnership rather than an occasional missions emphasis or special projects.

PARTNERSHIPS BUILT ON RELATIONSHIPS

Apart from personal relationships with missionaries, financial support is impersonal and programmatic. Volunteer projects seem designed for gratifying the church rather than for making an impact on a lost world. Promotional materials can inform churches about the needs and what others are doing, but a church's involvement is haphazard at best without a relationship with someone on the field.

Foundational to a sustained partnership is *prayer*—not occasional intercession for missionaries but consistent, fervent prayer for their families; their spiritual and physical health; their strategies; and the people among whom they work. Focused prayer requires an informed commitment. The church must train its members how to pray for mission strategies, how to be sensitive to security issues, and how to stay informed about unreached people groups and global developments. In addition, missionaries must be committed to the relationship with the church by providing regular, specific requests; communicating needs; and reporting on progress and struggles.

Projects are another practical way church members can get involved in missions and have a sense of ownership in the task. These can include collecting and shipping items needed by missionaries, mailing prayer letters, hosting a training event, creating a Web site, producing an advocacy video, and finding other ways to help at home. When projects are based on a sustained partnership, the church gains a sense of ownership in the mission objective of reaching a people group or a population segment. The volunteer trip is not an end in itself or something that diverts the missionary from his primary work; it becomes a key component of the ongoing field strategy. But if projects are to advance field strategy, they must be based on a relationship with the missionary and must be part of a long-term commitment.

A commitment to a *partnership* enables the church to become involved on the ground level of strategic planning with the missionary team. Instead of participating in volunteer trips as a string of mission projects without regard to the missionary's work, a church that has a partnership with a missionary has a better understanding of the needs and how its involvement in mission projects can supplement the missionary's work. Church members come to understand the barriers and the bridges within a specific culture and people group and can join missionary families on the field in a commitment to do whatever it takes to get the job done. This expanded perspective brings new resources and possibilities that the missionaries may not have envisioned or may not have had available otherwise.

Such a partnership is driven by a passion to see people evangelized and to see indigenous church-planting movements result. An ongoing partnership must be built on trust and respect. Deeper relationships take time to establish and maintain; they must be nurtured by communication, prayer, and commitment to a common objective.

What are three levels of involvement that describe what a church can do to nurture a relationship on the mission field and to participate in missions?

P_____ P_____ P_____

OTHER VALUABLE PARTNERSHIPS

Beyond the local church many Baptist state conventions and local Baptist associations have developed valuable partnerships in international missions. Rather than relegating the mission task to a denominational mission agency, these entities mobilize churches, promote mission support, and facilitate overseas involvement in a synergy of cooperation. While associations focus on local needs and state conventions equip churches to reach the people in their state, both recognize the importance of giving their churches a vision for the whole world by facilitating global involvement.

Missions reaches beyond where a person lives geographically and culturally. Just as churches lose their vitality when they become self-centered and inwardly focused, so do other entities when they neglect the larger mission task of mobilizing God's people to reach a lost world. Without the state conventions, the IMB would not be able to enlist the thousands of volunteers who are participating in evangelistic crusades, disaster relief, ministry projects, sports outreach, construction, medical work, and a multitude of other areas of witness around the world. The kingdom of God is advanced when state conventions, associations, and churches work together in partnership to reach the ends of the earth.

In the right column match what a church committed to kingdom growth will do with the defining function in the left column.

_____ 1. Seeking God's leadership   a. Telling

_____ 2. Sharing the gospel   b. Learning

_____ 3. Creating missions awareness   c. Going

_____ 4. Making plans and designating leadership   d. Multiplying

_____ 5. Facilitating church planting   e. Praying

_____ 6. Providing volunteer opportunities   f. Preparing

_____ 7. Calling out missionaries   g. Sending

_____ 8. Increasing financial support   h. Giving

1. Shawn Henricks, "Short-Term Mission Trips Spark Church's Passion for Missions," Baptist Press [online], 14 December 2005 [cited 10 January 2006]. Available from the Internet: www.bpnews.net.

Week 8

Reaching the Ends of the Earth

Daniel Peters is the city strategist for Madrid. Each week he mentors a leader from one of the three teams he oversees: the university student-ministry team, the Latin American mobilization team, and the immigrant-and-refugee team. He helps them develop a prayer strategy, study the culture and beliefs, and create a plan for reaching their people groups with the gospel. He also meets regularly with a Spanish friend who is not a believer. Peters leads another team that focuses on taking the gospel to Madrid's professionals. More than one million professionals live in Madrid, nearly 20 percent of the population, but fewer than ½ percent are Christians. "One large challenge here is not that people do not know about God," Peters says. "They are culturally religious people. They have many beautiful church buildings. However, I see millions of people here who often think religion and ritual are enough. I want them to experience that the only way to the Father is through a relationship with Jesus."[1]

How will we know when we have fulfilled the Great Commission? Jesus has already been preached in every country on our globe. However, millions of unreached people groups continue to live in darkness, weighted with sin. Many of the world's people groups arrive in America's cities every day. This week find out how you and your church can spread the gospel through different levels of involvement—some without leaving home! You will also rejoice at the many International Mission Board cooperative relationships that Southern Baptists join to actively pursue Jesus' Great Commission.

DAY 1
ADOPTING A KINGDOM WORLDVIEW

All of us view the world and life in general from the perspective of our own backgrounds and environments. What if we dared to allow God to reshape or enlarge our worldview? Could we identify with those whose world has been torn apart by genocide and ethnic conflicts in Rwanda, Bosnia, the Congo, Gaza, and Dagestan? If we lived among the thousands of Christian people groups in the Malukas of Indonesia, the tribal groups in Nigeria, and the Sudanese who are being massacred by Muslim fanatics, what would be our values and our view of life?

If our own country had the population density of India, three billion people would reside in the United States. What would that do to our economy, health-care plans, and perspective on comforts and entitlements we have taken for granted? Floods, earthquakes, typhoons, and drought become more frequent and commonplace throughout the world; they bring suffering and crisis to masses of people, paralyzing progress and destroying hope of development among impoverished third-world countries. How would you view life if you were one of more than one billion Muslims who are locked in a fatalistic view of eternity or if you were a Buddhist who thinks his destiny depends on accumulating karma or good deeds?

Because God has blessed us materially and has given us an abundance of resources, what do these Bible verses tell us to do?

Ephesians 4:28: _____

1 John 3:17: _____

Can you imagine God's worldview? He who created a diversity of people and societies views this spinning planet of more than six billion people. He sees those who are fortunate enough to have entered a redemptive relationship with Jesus Christ through repentance and faith. And then He sees the pain and suffering, the hunger and hopelessness, and the damning sin of the multitudes that are still separated from Him. If we are to be a kingdom people committed to kingdom growth, we need to reshape our worldview to see the world as God sees it.

GOD'S HEART FOR ALL PEOPLE

God has not given any church permission to draw a circle around its own community and say, "This is the extent of our responsibility." God's heart is for the whole world. If we are to be a church that exists to serve God's kingdom, we will realize that our mission task extends to all people. We are responsible to reach those of different languages and cultures within our cities; we share a responsibility with other churches to reach the unevangelized areas of our state and North America, but we also have a role in reaching the peoples of the world.

A kingdom worldview would reprioritize our lives and a stewardship of our resources. It would mean a commitment to pray specifically for the nations and peoples of the world. We would no longer focus our prayers exclusively on ourselves, our families, and those around us. Prayer warriors would be mobilized, and the Spirit of God would move burdened hearts from praying to action. With a broken heart we would intercede for those in darkness until barriers crumbled, doors opened, and the kingdom of God extended to the ends of the earth.

Giving would take on a new dimension. Church members would no longer see it as their personal prerogative to determine how much they give of their money. They would recognize that having a secure job and a steady income is God's blessing and that what they have belongs to Him. Their gifts to missions would be a decision of faith, under the lordship of Jesus Christ, trusting Him to provide for their needs as they give above and beyond their means.

First John 3:17 explains the motive for a kingdom worldview that results in our giving to those in need. What did John tell us about those who don't give? Circle your answer.

They don't love.   They are poor.   They don't care.   They are stingy.

A kingdom worldview will result in a church environment in which members regularly hear and respond to God's call to evangelize the whole world.

Read Matthew 9:36. How did Jesus describe people and Himself?

As _____ needing a _____

137

What does this verse tell us about Jesus' worldview? Underline your answer.

- He was concerned only about the people of Jerusalem.
- He had compassion for them but saw no hope for their future.
- His compassion led Him to act on their behalf.

GOD'S HEART FOR COOPERATION

Growing God's kingdom requires working cooperatively with other organizations and facilitating their involvement in reaching a lost world. IMB missionaries are spread rather thin, but we enhance the potential for extending the kingdom of God to the ends of the earth when we work together with others who are seeking to take the gospel to the nations. The work of the IMB is more effective, the global harvest is accelerated, a lost world hears the gospel, and the kingdom of God is advanced because state conventions, associations, and other stateside partners work together cooperatively.

*When we cease to be concerned about who gets credit
and who is in control, we will be amazed at what God will do among us.*

The IMB can report evangelistic harvests and church growth overseas because of effective partnerships with national conventions and churches with which we are affiliated. Spiritual breakthroughs are occurring on previously restricted fields because of a network of Great Commission agencies that are working together to address the lostness of our world. In fact, the greatest threat to our effectiveness is the tendency to take pride in what we have done rather than being humbled and recognizing that whatever we do derives from God's grace and blessing. We can be a part of a kingdom purpose that is bigger than ourselves.

A kingdom worldview focuses on God's purpose and glory. What does the Bible say about taking pride in our own efforts or accomplishments?

Proverbs 16:18: _____

Isaiah 42:8: _____

God will not share His glory. Those who work for recognition or seek to claim credit for what they have done will not receive the anointing of God's power. The amazing statistical growth of the numbers of lost people who have come into the kingdom in recent years can only be described as a movement of God, who desires to be exalted among all peoples.

DAY 2
COOPERATING WITH KINGDOM PARTNERS

God has raised within His body many diverse channels for addressing spiritual lostness—entities that are committed to the lordship of Jesus Christ, recognize Jesus as the exclusive and unique Savior of the world, and are committed to discipling the nations. In the same way God gives spiritual gifts to each member of the local church for the completeness of the body, He calls different organizations with unique gifts and ministries to work together in a synergy that will glorify Him and fulfill His mission of evangelizing the whole world.

> **Kingdom partnership:** *A cooperative effort among those who are committed to the authority of the Bible to fulfill the Great Commission and bring all peoples to saving faith in Jesus Christ*

GOD'S MISSION INCLUDES OTHERS

A few years ago a delegation from Wycliffe Bible Translators and the *Jesus* film project came to the IMB for a consultation. A spokesman from Wycliffe explained that they were accelerating Bible translation and in particular were focusing on quickly getting oral translations of the Gospel of Luke into as many languages as possible. This action was designed to resource the *Jesus* film project, which uses the Gospel of Luke as the text. The oral-translation effort would accelerate the production of this effective evangelistic tool in many more languages.

When asked why they were here, one in the group explained, "In the early stages of our partnership we realized that unless someone is deliberately engaged in starting churches, the results of our efforts will be rather limited. Having Scripture in their heart language and the *Jesus* film graphically portraying the gospel—especially among oral cultures—is valuable, but the lasting benefit will not be significant without following up new believers and starting indigenous churches." He continued, "No organization is as focused and effective in church planting as the International Mission Board. Unless you are willing to cooperate in partnership with us, our vision cannot be fulfilled." The statement was significant. Our unique contribution to reaching a lost world was recognized, and our church-planting efforts had a reputation for effectiveness among other evangelical groups.

Why is cooperation with others an expression of a kingdom worldview?

The IMB became affiliated with the Evangelical Fellowship of Mission Agencies in 1995. The EFMA includes about 120 diverse mission agencies. Many are rather small and specialized, but others—both denominational and parachurch organizations—are quite large. I was humbled to realize that God had enabled us to contribute to kingdom growth as part of a vast array of mission organizations and agencies.

THE CHALLENGE OF ORAL CULTURES

As evangelical organizations began to focus on the Last Frontier people groups who had yet to hear and respond to the gospel, an amazing reality surfaced. Most of these people groups were oral cultures, consisting of people who could not read or understand the Bible and evangelistic literature even if it had been available in their language. As a result, many of them remained unreached. Because most of our mission strategies are geared to the Bible and use the written Word for discipleship, leadership training, and church planting, we found that we were ill equipped for reaching these illiterate people groups.

Chronological Bible storying could be used to share the gospel, but how could discipleship and the training that are needed for church-planting movements take place? The challenge was bigger than any one organization, but four of the largest mission agencies found themselves at the forefront of meeting this need. The IMB, Campus Crusade for Christ, Wycliffe Bible Translators, and Youth with a Mission were all significantly engaging oral cultures and people groups. Working together in an effort that has come to be called OneStory, we are developing oral materials and sharing them for discipleship and leadership training, based on the narrative approach of chronological Bible storying. This joint venture avoids duplication, provides materials for people groups all over the world, and serves other mission groups through these cooperative efforts.

Cooperation requires us neither to compromise our doctrinal positions nor to sacrifice our convictions about methodology, because cooperation and unity are not ends in themselves. Cooperating with others provides a utilitarian approach to accomplish a mutual objective. Parameters must exist in any partnership, but when various organizations come together seeking to overcome the lostness of unreached people groups, a synergy can result that makes the gospel known on a broader scale than if someone were trying to do it alone.

In contrast, ecumenism implies an organic unity in which each participating entity gives up something for the sake of unity. Southern Baptists would never value unity over doctrinal convictions based on the inerrant Word of God. We would never compromise essential matters of faith for a utilitarian objective. But cooperation with others can provide an opportunity for doctrinal influence and leadership among others.

Jesus film / bible in language

Draw lines across the columns to match the words on the left
with their descriptions on the right.

- Cooperation
- Compromise
- Unity

- Gives up a conviction to work with others
- Never valued over doctrinal convictions
- A utilitarian approach to a common goal

FIVE LEVELS OF PARTNERSHIP

The IMB has defined five levels of partnership with other mission organizations. Level 1 is the most superficial; it aims to gain *initial access* to a people group or a population segment. Cooperation may be with a local university or medical facility that has no Christian or religious identification but provides access to a previously closed country. Links with secular humanitarian organizations and multinational corporations may also be utilized.

Five Levels of Partnership

use medical to get into a closed country

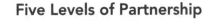

LEVEL 5
LEVEL 4
LEVEL 3
LEVEL 2
LEVEL 1

Level 2 takes the next strategic step to *ministry*. Cooperation at this level opens the door to the gospel and makes an impact on society. Enlisting prayer for a people group or a city, responding to a natural disaster, addressing chronic famine, and providing pure drinking water are actions that can make an impact at this level. The partnership may include anyone who wishes to address these needs and is equipped to contribute to meeting them.

Level 3 takes the partnership beyond prayer advocacy, humanitarian projects, or involvement with government and secular institutions to a point of *gospel presentation*. Therefore, partners at this level must be defined by those committed to New Testament evangelism. The number of potential partner organizations is greatly reduced to those who are devoted to presenting Jesus Christ as the exclusive way of salvation and who believe the only hope for eternal life is through coming to Him in repentance and faith as Savior and Lord.

Level 4 moves beyond evangelism and proclamation to *church planting*. At this level the scope of potential partners is limited to those whose beliefs are compatible with Baptist doctrine. At level 5 the missionary seeks to create *ongoing structures and institutions* that will shape the future of Christianity among a people and ensure its continuing extension.

The task of discipling the nations and peoples of the world must be carried out in harmony with other evangelical believers rather than in isolation. To work independently in exclusion of others would not mean greater effectiveness. It would marginalize Southern Baptists from being aligned with much of what God is doing in the world.

God's kingdom is bigger than Southern Baptists, and while we hold firmly and without compromise to *The Baptist Faith and Message,* cooperation with the efforts of others is accelerating kingdom growth, especially in places that have not previously had access to the gospel. Such cooperation must not infringe on the autonomy of mission partners in following God's leadership and our accountability to Southern Baptists. Cooperation must be based on mutual trust and commitment to a common biblical objective.

Define a Great Commission partnership at each of the following levels.

Level 1: _____

Level 2: _____

Level 3: _____

Level 4: _____

Level 5: _____

DAY 3
REACHING THE WORLD THAT HAS COME TO US

An amazing reverse impact in mission strategies occurs when churches begin to discover that the unevangelized people groups they are seeking to reach overseas actually live in their own cities. A small church in Illinois adopted a people group in South Asia. Then they became aware that Asian Indians operated motels and worked in fast-food restaurants in the vicinity of their church. They were startled to discover that a sizeable community of their adopted people group lived in the area. The church began Bible studies, and they soon found themselves part of a global mission strategy without having to leave home. Another church worked with a nonresidential strategy coordinator to pray for access to an Iranian people group. They began to connect with an expatriate community of this people group residing in California.

Representatives of most west-African people groups can be found in New York City. Churches focusing on these peoples have been an asset to the missionaries on the field. As these churches have shared the gospel with those who are in the States, new west-African believers spread the good news to relatives and friends in their homeland.

Most unreached people groups around the world live in places that are restricted, where it is difficult to proclaim the gospel openly. Practically all of them have people from their group who live in the United States, where there is no restriction on witnessing. When churches have a vision for reaching people groups here, they find that the relationships these people have with families in their home countries become conduits for the gospel to flow to the nations.

DISCIPLING THE NATIONS

We tend to distort the Great Commission when we think that Jesus' mandate to disciple the nations refers only to foreign countries. Therefore, we see the words as parallel to the "ends of the earth" segment of the Acts 1:8 paradigm. *The nations*—or *ta ethne*—in Matthew 28:19 means *the peoples,* or ethnolinguistic people groups wherever they live. This meaning of *nations* was recognized in the history of our own country as we traditionally referred to Native Americans as the Sioux nation or the Cherokee nation.

> List ethnic groups in your city or state who represent different people groups who have lived in our country for generations.

We are to reach and disciple the diverse people groups in our Jerusalem, Judea, and Samaria, as well as around the world. Your city, state, and country are made up of many nations and peoples with different languages, cultures, traditions, and worldviews. But churches tend to focus on reaching their own kind of people while leaving the task of evangelizing other races and languages to mission entities.

Jesus explained to His disciples in Luke 24:46-47 that His death and resurrection would provide a message of redemption for all nations or all peoples. Acts 1:8 is not a sequential progression of reaching our own kind of people and then extending our witness to the surrounding territory. Jesus modeled Acts 1:8 when He ministered geographically and cross-culturally to people who were different, such as the Samaritans. We are to disciple the ethnolinguistic peoples in our city and those who live around us, as well as those who live overseas.

Researchers report that Hispanics are the fastest-growing ethnic group in America. The growth of this population segment, including the massive influx of legal and illegal alien laborers from Latin America as well as other international immigrants, will replace Anglo-Americans as the majority in the United States in the not-too-distant future. The demographics of cities and neighborhoods are changing. Most urban areas are characterized by sections populated exclusively by Vietnamese, Chinese, Koreans, Arabs, or others. Signs on stores and billboards are in foreign languages. Mosques and Hindu temples are being built alongside our churches.

Native Americans and African-Americans have long been a predominant part of our American society. Don't all of these people groups need Jesus? Does our Great Commission responsibility extend to people in our own neighborhood? Can we go on mission trips to foreign countries and take pride in sending missionaries to the nations abroad while ignoring the nations that reside among us?

> List nationalities, people groups, and religious adherents who live in your city or geographic region but are not native to America.

Beyond someone's adopted people group, multitudes of international students, tourists, and immigrant workers from around the world are flooding into the United States. More than six hundred thousand students come from abroad each year to study in American colleges and universities. As the brightest and best, they will become the government and business leaders of the future and will influence their countries' societies and policies.

How tragic that they could spend four to six years in our country and never be invited to a church or have the opportunity to meet a Christian family. In almost every city multitudes of foreigners are lonely and desperate for friendship and encouragement. They are often shunned by most Americans because of their strange dress or deficient language skills. Yet we sometimes spend thousands of dollars to cover the cost of a brief volunteer mission trip to exotic places while ignoring the world that has come to our doorstep.

THE NATIONS ARE HERE

In Acts 2 we read the account of Peter's sermon and the witness of the apostles on the Day of Pentecost. A number of ethnic people groups from around the world are listed; in fact, verse 5 says that "devout men from every nation under heaven" were in Jerusalem, and they heard the gospel in their own language. Why should the disciples have been so amazed? Just a short time earlier Jesus had told them that they were to disciple the nations.

It was as if Jesus were saying, "This is what I was talking about. I have brought them to you. I have demonstrated the power of the gospel to save them; now go to the ends of the earth and be My witnesses to all peoples." Maybe we aren't going overseas in the numbers that we should, but God is bringing the world to us. A church that has a global vision will not neglect the peoples God has brought within the shadow of their own church—into their Jerusalem—from the ends of the earth.

Is your church seeking to share the gospel with other ethnic, racial, or language groups in your city? ❑ Yes ❑ No

What are some ways you and your church can bridge cultural and language gaps to befriend members of other people groups?

_____

_____

_____

Remember that these relationships must go beyond friendships to opportunities to share the gospel. If you present yourself to God for His use as a witness, He will bring you opportunities to share His love for every person and nation.

DAY 4
IMPLEMENTING A CHURCH-BASED STRATEGY

Churches that have provided opportunities for volunteer mission trips, encouraged giving to missions, prayed for unreached people groups, and called out missionaries have found that they become more effective in local growth and outreach. Oswald Smith, a former pastor of the strong, mission-minded Peoples Church in Toronto, is credited with having said, "The light that shines the farthest shines the brightest at home." If a church is involved in shining the light of the gospel to the ends of the earth, a big, powerful fire of evangelism must be burning among its people at home.

Place an X on the line to represent your own personal fire of evangelism.

Barely a glimmer   Burning   Burning brightly

One church that has experienced a phenomenal increase in membership and baptisms marks the beginning of its growth at the point when members began to go on overseas mission trips. As each new family joins the church, they are encouraged to get a passport because they will want to get involved in the exciting flow of mission projects around the world. At their current rate of increasing involvement in missions, the church envisions having a volunteer team somewhere overseas every week of the year. Every Sunday they pray for a team on the mission field and commission another group that is preparing to go!

Another church with fewer than one thousand members has seen 72 career missionaries commissioned from its fellowship in the past 10 years. One pastor testified to the radical new dimension of stewardship that has resulted from missions involvement by his congregation: "When I became pastor 20 years ago, we struggled to give $1,000 a year to the Cooperative Program; now we are giving $1,000 a day! We have never had a problem meeting our local budget since we started giving priority to missions!"

LEVELS OF MISSIONS INVOLVEMENT

Most churches are conscientious about their mission task but have been nurtured in a legacy of fulfilling their mission responsibility by supporting missionaries. About 70 percent of Southern Baptist churches participate in missions only through giving financial support to the Cooperative Program and mission offerings. They support the work of the state convention and mission boards, but they have not envisioned any involvement beyond simply being *supporting churches.* However, many have discovered opportunities for involvement with missionaries and in strategies that reach beyond their local church programs. Identified as *awakening churches,* these have taken the initiative to sponsor occasional mission trips and volunteer mission projects for their members.

Others are *moving-and-growing churches* in missions involvement. A high priority is given to mission projects, not as a one-time experience but as a continuing partnership with an overseas missionary or in a pioneer area of the United States. An increased utilization of media resources and information enhances the knowledge and awareness of what God is doing around the world; an effort is made to mobilize church members' widespread participation.

A significant number of churches are not just moving and growing with regard to awareness and participation in missions but have developed to the level of *strategic involvement.* These churches have adopted missionaries and people groups or have made a commitment to a city or an area in another part of the country. They have aligned with the IMB's or the North American Mission Board's field strategies to do whatever they can to see a city, people group, or population segment successfully evangelized and churches planted. Their people have embraced a missions lifestyle in their giving and sacrificial personal involvement in fulfilling the mission of the church. They exhibit a passionate commitment to intercessory prayer for their mission target in the United States and overseas. They maintain a consistent level of communication as partners with field missionaries.

A few churches have moved to a higher dimension of involvement as *strategic mobilizers.* These churches have developed a sense of ownership and partnership with an area of the world, a strategic-focus city, or a cluster of people groups. They have become advocates for mission strategies among other churches. Sometimes referred to as hub churches, they are taking responsibility on behalf of the missionaries to publish and disseminate advocacy materials, enlist other churches, and train and facilitate them to be involved in the mission task.

Supporting churches: *Churches that support the state convention and the mission boards financially*

Awakening churches: *Churches that sponsor occasional mission trips and volunteer mission projects for their members*

Moving-and-growing churches: *Churches that give high priority to missions involvement through a continuing partnership with an overseas missionary or in a pioneer area of the United States*

Strategic-involvement churches: *Churches that have partnered with missionaries and adopted people groups or have made a commitment to see a city, people group, or population segment successfully evangelized and churches planted*

Strategic mobilizers: *Churches that take responsibility on behalf of missionaries to publish and disseminate advocacy materials, enlist other churches, and train and facilitate them to be involved in the mission task*

Circle your church's level of missions involvement.
Supporting   Awakening   Moving and growing
Strategically involved   Strategic mobilizers

Churches Reaching the Ends of the Earth

No clear delineation among these categories is intended. The point is that a church can plug into missions at any point. Wherever a church finds itself in its level of interest and commitment, its involvement can continue to grow. In fact, continuing development of participation in missions is inevitable. I have often likened volunteer mission trips to an advertisement for potato chips. The slogan of the ad was "You can't eat just one!" Once members have been on a mission trip, have seen the needs of a lost world, and have discovered how God can use them, they have to go back. The passion is contagious among the rest of the congregation, and participation grows into a sense of ownership for reaching a lost world.

What does your church need to do or what must happen for it to move to the next level of missions involvement?

_____

_____

BUSINESS AND PROFESSIONAL OPPORTUNITIES

Obviously, most church members do not sense God's call to become missionaries. But that doesn't exempt them from involvement in God's kingdom task. Every Christian can pray, give, and/or participate in volunteer mission projects. Some can contribute even more to reaching the ends of the earth. As the speed and convenience of transportation and communication grow, more business enterprises are becoming global. Commerce is no longer characterized by local or even national markets. Manufacturing components are produced all over the world.

Developing countries, as new players in the global economy, yearn for guidance and training. Multinational businesses have been the channel through which thousands of Southern Baptists have found themselves on overseas assignments. An estimated 24,000 Southern Baptists a year travel to China on business. Many isolate themselves with their American colleagues in an expatriate community, but kingdom professionals project themselves into the midst of the culture, building relationships with local clients and partners who need Christ. Their contacts with government officials and influential business persons have helped create a better understanding of the Christian faith and have reduced hostilities and restrictions for local believers and missionaries.

What can business persons and professionals who are not called as full-time missionaries do to advance God's kingdom around the world?

_____

_____

DAY 5
A COMMITMENT TO KINGDOM IMPACT

When my wife and I were married just after finishing college, our commitment to missions was already solidified. Some of our friends jokingly said our passion for missions bordered on being obnoxious! We were probably a little condescending when we questioned whether others were really saved if they had never considered the possibility of missionary service. Nevertheless, there was no question of our calling and our kingdom perspective when we had our BSU choir sing "O Zion, Haste" as the recessional at our wedding. I will never forget going out of the church sanctuary together to the challenge of the refrain:

> *Publish glad tidings, tidings of peace,*
> *Tidings of Jesus, redemption and release.*[2]

That was the purpose to which we devoted our marriage and our lives. However, I never paid much attention to the other words of that hymn until both of my children, their spouses, and our grandchildren left for the mission field. The third verse suddenly took on new meaning:

> Give of thy sons to bear the message glorious;
> Give of thy wealth to speed them on their way;
> Pour out thy soul for them in pray'r victorious;
> And all thou spendest Jesus will repay.[3]

It takes a special commitment for parents and families to give their children and grandchildren to the Lord, but we need to realize that they belong to Him. What greater joy than to know God has chosen them for kingdom service! A commitment to kingdom growth means that more men, women, and young people will respond to the call to go. We will give generously to provide their support and pour out our souls in prayer that through them our Lord Jesus will be glorified to the ends of the earth.

FAITHFUL TO THE END

Does empowering kingdom growth to the ends of the earth have anything to do with end times and Christ's return? As already noted, Jesus said in Matthew 24:14, "'This good news of the kingdom will be proclaimed in all the world as a testimony to all nations. And then the end will come.'" My frequent reference to this verse has led some to presume that Christ's second coming serves as the impetus for mission efforts to reach all the world with the gospel. Many people are interpreting contemporary global events as biblical prophecy and monitoring conflict in the Middle East to predict the end times. The signs of Christ's coming will continue to be prolific, creating more and more speculation.

Although I believe in our Lord's personal, bodily return at any time, I have never been concerned about the timing of that glorious event. God calls us to proclaim His salvation, and we are simply to walk in faithfulness and obedience in the task to which He calls us as His people. In fact, Jesus said to His disciples when asked about the timing of His return in Acts 1:7-8, "'It is not for you to know times or periods that the Father has set by His own authority. But ... you will be My witnesses ... to the ends of the earth.'"

No one but the Father knows when the second coming will occur. The time of that event is not to be our concern. Our focus is to proclaim the gospel where we live and to the ends of the earth; yet Jesus made clear that global evangelization will precede the end. I would never presume to interpret God's criteria for determining when the gospel has been preached to all peoples, but it is evident that we are living in an era when Jesus' words are being fulfilled.

Every country on earth has been penetrated with a Christian witness. People groups who have never heard of Jesus are systematically being touched by the gospel. Evangelistic tools and innovative strategies are being implemented in places that would have been unimaginable just a few years ago. Unprecedented progress is being made in giving all peoples an opportunity to hear, understand, and respond to the gospel.

WHAT IS AMERICA'S SPIRITUAL CONDITION?

As I share testimonies and report on kingdom advances overseas, I am often asked why we don't see these kinds of things happening in America. Why are our churches plateaued and ineffective? Why are indifference and spiritual lethargy the norm? In spite of prolific numbers of churches and our history of Christian witness, why do we seem to make little impact on society while our nation continues on a moral slide and Christian values diminish? I haven't had an answer to these questions and have personally been disturbed by these observations. These conditions are not unexpected in other cultures. There we are confronted with the tragedy of those in spiritual darkness where the gospel is not known. But what is the explanation in our own country?

As I have examined Scripture, I have gained some insight into a possible explanation. Israel had become God's chosen people, not because they deserved His favor but so that they would be a people through whom God could fulfill His mission. He blessed them, not for their benefit but to be a priestly nation as

> *"a light for the nations*
> *to be My salvation to the ends of the earth"* (Isa. 49:6).

When Jesus gave the Great Commission to His followers, did they get it? Did they move out in obedience to follow His purpose in carrying the gospel to Judea, cross-culturally to Samaria, and to the ends of the earth? No, they stayed in Jerusalem until God allowed persecution to come in order for the believers to be dispersed, carrying the gospel with them (see Acts 8:1).

Throughout the Old Testament we read of God's allowing Israel to be conquered and punished by pagan tribes. We usually observe that it was because they forsook God to worship idols and other gods. But were not their defeat and the subsequent consequences the result of their disobedience to fulfill God's purpose of glorifying Him among the nations? Instead of leading those around them to know God, they compromised and conformed to the cultural worldviews in which they lived. Instead of focusing on extending God's kingdom and proclaiming His glory among the nations, they became self-centered, concerned only for their own welfare and blessings.

Paul observed in Romans that because the hearts of the Jews had become hardened, they were rejected "until the full number of the Gentiles [the nations] has come in" (Rom. 11:25). Israel was disobedient in following God because its eyes had become blind to God's purpose. God's people became self-centered, focusing on themselves and their special status instead of their mission to reach the nations. Their hearts were hardened toward God and toward the peoples in darkness to whom they were supposed to be witnesses.

Could it be that God's blessings and anointing will be withheld until we regain a vision for our purpose as the people of God? To what extent must God allow our nation to suffer and our churches to flounder before we begin to look beyond our own programs and interests to our larger kingdom mission?

If all peoples of the world are to know Him and God's kingdom is to be extended to the ends of the earth, we, the spiritual descendants of Abraham, must obey. May we not follow the example of Israel, who became blind to God's purpose and whose hearts were hardened toward God and a lost world. Let us be obedient as His instrument for kingdom growth.

> What commitment(s) is God leading you to make in order to be personally involved in kingdom growth? Check all that apply.
> ❑ To be open to God's call to missionary service
> ❑ To give more generously and sacrificially to missions
> ❑ To be more conscientious about witnessing to different cultures locally
> ❑ To lead my church to be more aware of and better informed about missions
> ❑ To be willing to participate in a volunteer mission project overseas
> ❑ To consider enlisting and leading a volunteer mission team
> ❑ To be open to my children and grandchildren going as missionaries
> ❑ To pray daily for missionaries whom I know and for specific people groups

1. Brittany Connor, "Missionary Kids in Madrid Expand Their Parents' Outreach," Baptist Press [online], 13 December 2005 [cited 9 January 2006]. Available from the Internet: *www.bpnews.net*. Name changed for security reasons.
2. Mary Ann Thomson, "O Zion, Haste," *The Baptist Hymnal* (Nashville: Convention Press, 1991), 583.
3. Ibid.

INTRODUCTORY SESSION

Session Goals

After this session members will be able to—

- summarize the purpose of this study;
- identify benefits of participating in this study;
- define *evangelism;*
- identify the IMB's purpose;
- state the requirements for completing this study.

Before the Session

1. Purchase copies of this workbook for participants well in advance by writing to LifeWay Church Resources Customer Service; One LifeWay Plaza; Nashville, TN 37234-0113; phoning toll free (800) 458-2772; ordering online at *www.lifeway.com;* faxing (615) 251-5933; or visiting the LifeWay Christian Store serving you.

2. Read the contents pages (pp. 3–4) and "About This Study" on page 6. Then read all eight weeks of content to get an overview of the study.

3. Examine the remaining sessions in this leader guide to identify any advance preparation you need to make.

During the Session

1. Welcome members. State the purpose of the course, using "About This Study," page 6, and the information gleaned from your overview of the content.

2. Ask members to name benefits they expect to receive from this course.

3. Distribute copies of this workbook and ask members to examine the diagram on page 38. Point out the number of people who are lost with little or no access to the gospel, the number of people who are lost with only limited access to the gospel, the number of cultural Christians, and the number of evangelical believers in the world.

4. Ask two members to read Matthew 28:19-20 and Acts 1:8. State that Jesus commanded His church to share the gospel with everyone—to the ends of the earth.

5. Ask volunteers to define *evangelism.* Then share the definition on page 37. Ask, How does the IMB help Southern Baptist churches carry out Jesus' command to reach the ends of the earth? Explain that the IMB exists to provide all people an opportunity to hear, understand, and respond to the gospel. This study will teach us how to strategize with the IMB to make an impact on the world.

6. Direct members to week 1 (p. 7). Explain that the study consists of eight weeks and that each week is divided into five daily segments of reading and activities. Emphasize that members should complete each daily study and the learning activities in order to learn and apply the material. State that Christian Growth Study Plan credit is available for those who complete the study. See page 175.

7. Ask members to read week 1 and to complete the learning activities before the next session. Close with prayer.

Session 1
Discovering God's Kingdom Purpose

Session Goals

After this session members will be able to—

- define *kingdom of God;*
- identify four mission fields to which believers are called;
- summarize key Scriptures that articulate our mission task;
- define *people group* and explain how Scripture expresses our mission task in terms of people groups;
- describe the IMB's role in facilitating the global advance of God's kingdom.

Before the Session

1. Study week 1 and complete the activities.
2. Be prepared to show DVD segment 1.
3. Write each of the following Scripture references on a separate slip of paper: *Genesis 12:3; Psalm 22:27-28; Psalm 67:1-2; Psalm 96:2-3; Isaiah 49:6; Romans 10:13-14.*
4. Prepare a placard with the IMB's vision statement on page 20.

During the Session

1. Show DVD segment 1.
2. Write the phrase *kingdom of God* on a dry-erase board and ask volunteers to define it as you record their ideas. Use the material in day 1 to clarify the meaning. Lead members to discuss the implications of Christ's lordship for individual believers, our church, our community, and our nation. Lead them to discuss what these elements of our society would be like if God's kingdom were extended to all the world. Consider world peace, openness to the gospel, ethnic warfare, church conflicts, social evils, and human relationships.

3. Assign members to read the following Scripture passages and to state what the verses imply about the kingdom of God.

- Exodus 19:4-6 (Obedience to God and submission to His lordship will guarantee protection as God's possession, will make us holy, and will enable us to serve as priests to represent Him and bring others to know Him.)

- Matthew 3:2 (As Jesus came to make the kingdom of God a reality, we must repent to gain access and become a part of the kingdom.)

- Matthew 6:10 (We should pray for God's kingdom to come on earth by allowing His will to be done in our lives.)

- Matthew 24:14 (As followers of Jesus, we are to proclaim His kingdom to all the world and among all peoples; this will precede His return.)

- Matthew 13:18-21 (God's kingdom begins small, but its nature is to grow; like leaven permeating bread dough, its influence is to permeate all of life and society.)

4. Ask: How is the kingdom to grow quantitatively? (Through our witness and mission efforts to proclaim the gospel

of the kingdom, win others to Jesus, and plant churches among all peoples) How is the kingdom to grow qualitatively? (By allowing Jesus to be the Lord of our lives, influencing society toward Christian principles, and discipling new believers) How are these two types of growth related? (Each one produces the other. If Christ is the Lord of our lives, we will witness; if He reigns in our church, we will reach out. If the kingdom is growing in number and area, churches should disciple and nurture believers in a sanctified life of service that glorifies God and reflects the reality of His reign.) Why is the local church God's primary agent for kingdom growth? (Local bodies of believers nurture and disciple new converts to live in obedience to Christ's lordship; they are the massive grassroots points where God's people can have an impact on a lost world.)

5. Direct members to the final activity in day 1 (p. 11) and ask them to identify the geographic area and the denominational entity that serves and facilitates the church in its kingdom witness. (*Jerusalem*— immediate city or town, local association; *Judea*—state, state convention; *Samaria*— North America and cross-cultural witness, North American Mission Board; *ends of the earth*—other nations and peoples, IMB)

6. Ask three volunteers to read Matthew 28:19-20; Mark 16:15; and Acts 1:8. Emphasize that Matthew 28:19-20 tells us to "make disciples of all nations"; Mark 16:15 tells us to "preach [proclaim] the gospel to the whole creation [everyone everywhere]"; and Acts 1:8 says we have received the Holy Spirit's power in order to be witnesses in our immediate community, in the surrounding area outside our community, in neighboring geographic areas and cross-culturally to other ethnic peoples, and to all nations and peoples throughout the world.

7. Read Isaiah 6:1-8. Ask members to name the items they marked in the activity on page 13. (Correct: 2, 3, 4, 6) Ask volunteers to name what they are passionate about. Challenge members to open their hearts to allowing God to make reaching lost people the passion of their lives.

8. Ask a volunteer to define *people group*. (Different languages, cultures, and ethnic groups) Ask members to react to the fact that *nations* in the traditional understanding of the Great Commission does not refer to countries but to people groups. Ask, What are some barriers to reaching people groups? (Language, geography, ethnicity, values)

9. Call for answers to the activity on page 18). (*Nations:* Nigeria, Korea, Brazil, India, Iraq. *Languages:* Spanish, Mandarin, Swahili, Arabic, Hindi. *People groups:* Han Chinese, Navajo, K'etchi, Egyptian, Tamil.)

10. Divide members into six groups and give each group one of the assignment slips you prepared. Ask the groups to read the assigned Scripture and to discuss how it expresses our mission task in terms of people groups and every segment of society.

Allow time for group work; then call for reports. Summarize, God's purpose and desire are for all peoples to be discipled and to become a part of His kingdom.

11. State that these clear scriptural mandates of God's purpose and mission for His people provide the basis for the IMB's vision statement. Display and read the placard you prepared. Explain that reaching all peoples is not our mission; it is God's mission, and He is at work in the world to evangelize all peoples. Our task is to join Him in what He is doing. Clarify that the IMB's responsibility is not to do missions on behalf of Southern Baptists; the Great Commission was given to every church, believer, and denominational entity. The IMB exists to facilitate, serve, and enable all Southern Baptists to obey the Great Commission. Ask a volunteer to distinguish between *mission* and *missions*. (See p. 12.)

12 Ask volunteers to share the visions they wrote in the activity on page 22. State, God has a vision for reaching all peoples. Ask, Why is a vision for an evangelized world necessary to motivate us to be an instrument of kingdom growth? (A vision keeps us focused on our purpose so that we aren't diverted to less important tasks.) State, God's vision and our vision for the world are expressed in Revelation 7:9. Ask a member to read that verse. Then say, When Christ returns, there will be a multitude no one can count that represents every nation, tribe, people, and language.

13. Explain the threefold paradigm shift in the IMB's strategy of leading churches to fulfill their mission task.

• *Personalization* instead of generic support. Churches are to be personally and directly involved in on-the-field strategies around the world. Missions is not simply giving to support others for the task without knowing who they are, what they are doing, and how God is at work. Churches should own a specific segment of the task.

• *Partnership* instead of exclusive control. Churches are not to see missionaries as fulfilling churches' mission responsibilities. Church and denominational partners are to own the task and add resources and involvement that will produce a synergy of results rather than expecting missionaries to control everything that is done overseas.

• *Passion* instead of program promotion. The motivation for missions must come from a passion for God and from having His heart for the nations rather than promoting a program or project, placing guilt on people, or soliciting their involvement from a sense of obligation.

14. Ask whether anyone has adopted a new personal vision for extending God's kingdom to the ends of the earth or a new vision for their church's involvement in missions.

15. Ask members to read week 2 and to complete the learning activities before the next session. Close with prayer.

SESSION 2
GROWING GOD'S KINGDOM THROUGH MISSIONS

Session Goals

After this session members will be able to—

- identify what Scripture says about people who are without Christ;
- reaffirm their belief that Jesus is the only provision for salvation;
- state what is necessary to be saved;
- define *evangelism* and *discipleship;*
- explain the necessity of planting churches to extend God's kingdom;
- identify global events that God uses to draw people to Himself.

Before the Session

1. Read week 2 and complete the activities.
2. Be prepared to show DVD segment 2.
3. Prepare a placard with the IMB's basic belief on page 26.
4. Enlist two members to define *evangelism* and *discipleship,* using the material in day 4.
5. Prepare a placard with the IMB's basic task on page 40.
6. Have available a world map or globe. A world map can be ordered from *www.imb.org.*

During the Session

1. Show DVD segment 2. Refer to the world's lost. Ask: Do you agree that most who died in the Asian tsunami in December 2004 were lost? Why? Does the huge number of lost people cause us to rationalize away their lostness and hopelessness?

2. Ask five members to read aloud the following verses and to summarize what they say about the spiritual condition of people without Christ: John 3:18; Romans 3:23; 6:23; 10:1-2; Ephesians 1:1-2.

3. Display the placard you prepared with the IMB's basic belief. Ask: Do you agree with this statement? Should this be an impetus for missions? Why or why not?

4. Ask two members to read aloud 2 Corinthians 4:6 and Isaiah 60:1-3 and point out the Bible's frequent use of light and darkness for salvation and lostness. Ask: What is the switch that turns on the light? (The story of Jesus—the gospel) Why is a simple story the most effective tool for making an impact on lostness? (The Spirit of God indwells the message of the gospel; the truth that Jesus is God's Son, who died for the sins of the world, is the knowledge that someone needs to be saved.) Who is responsible for telling that story? (Everyone who knows it) Ask, Can someone be saved other than through personal faith in Jesus Christ? (No) Ask two members to read aloud John 14:6 and Acts 4:12.

5. Review the true/false activity on page 33. (1. F, 2. F, 3. F, 4. F, 5. F, 6. T, 7. F, 8. F, 9. T)

6. Ask volunteers to share their answers to the activity on page 36.

7. Call on the two members you enlisted to define *evangelism* and *discipleship* from the

material in day 4. Draw attention to the diagram on page 38. Ask: Can missionaries reach the massive numbers of lost people? (No) How can the multitudes be reached? (By making disciples and establishing churches) Show the placard you prepared with the IMB's basic task. Explain the meaning of *indigenous.* (Originating from within the local context) Ask, Why is it important for evangelism to result in churches? (Because new believers become a part of a fellowship in which they can be discipled, encouraged, and grow and through which they can witness and serve God. It becomes a nucleus of expanded witness and evangelism.) State, For the kingdom to grow, the goal must be making disciples, not just winning converts.

8. Direct members to the activity on page 43. Ask members to identify any listed countries they had never heard of. Call on volunteers to identify their locations as you point these out on a world map or globe. (*Uzbekistan*—in central Asia above Afghanistan and below Kazakhstan, formerly part of the Soviet Union; *Bosnia-Herzegovina*—on the eastern side of the Adriatic Sea, once part of Yugoslavia; *Chechnya*—a central Asian republic northwest of the Caspian Sea, part of the Russian Republic; *Chad*— a large sub-Saharan country between west and central Africa; *Azerbaijan*—in central Asia on the western coast of the Caspian Sea, formerly part of the Soviet Union; *Bhutan*—a small Buddhist country east of Nepal and north of India;

Slovenia—formerly part of Yugoslavia in southeastern Europe; *Guinea-Bissau*— a small west-African country on the coast south of Senegal) Emphasize that these and many other places we may not have heard of need to hear the gospel. God loves and died to save these people.

9. Ask, What global events might God be using in His providence to fulfill His redemptive mission? (The decline of Communism, the emergence of China as a world economic power, ethnic conflict and disintegration of national powers, natural disasters, terrorist activity, turmoil in the Middle East, economic instability, advanced technology and communication, multinational business enterprises, the Internet, postmodern defiance of biblical authority) State: In these times of political disruptions, social upheaval, economic deterioration, wars, and natural disasters, God is creating an environment in which people cannot look to their culture, traditions, and religion but only to our Lord Jesus Christ for salvation and hope. God has called us to His kingdom for such a time as this. His mission will be fulfilled. His kingdom will grow until it embraces representatives from all nations and peoples—every tribe and language group. The only question is whether we will be faithful and obedient to join God in the task to which He calls us as His people.

10. Ask members to read week 3 and to complete the learning activities before the next session. Close with prayer.

SESSION 3
EMPOWERING GOD'S KINGDOM THROUGH PRAYER

Session Goals

After this session members will be able to—

- state two commitments that are essential to receiving God's power for the mission task;
- define *incarnational witness* and explain why placing personnel on the mission field is an essential IMB strategy;
- evaluate the proportion of missionaries to Southern Baptists and assess our ability to support more missionaries;
- identify ways to pray for and financially support missionaries.

Before the Session

1. Read week 3 and complete the activities.
2. Be prepared to show DVD segment 3.
3. Write these references on separate slips of paper: *Matthew 28:18-20; Acts 1:8; Romans 15:18-19.* Give the slips to three members as they arrive. Ask them to read their assigned verses and to be prepared to identify what they say about God's power for missions.
4. Prepare a placard with the IMB's basic commitment on page 47. Prepare a placard with the IMB's basic strategy on page 50.
5. Have three large sheets of paper and three markers available for group work.
6. Enlist a member to visit the IMB's Web site, *www.imb.org,* and to be prepared to report briefly on resources for praying for and encouraging missionaries.

7. Enlist a member to prepare to report on PRAYERPlus Partnerships, using the material in day 4.
8. Find the answers to these questions: What amount did your church give to missions through the Lottie Moon Christmas Offering® for International Missions last year? How much was that per member? What percentage of the annual budget does your church designate to God's work through the Cooperative Program?

During the Session

1. Show DVD segment 3.
2. Call on the designated members to read their assigned Scriptures and to identify what they say about God's power.
3. Display the placard you prepared with the IMB's basic commitment. Ask members why each commitment is essential to receiving God's power. (Without a commitment to the lordship of Jesus Christ, we are working in our own power and strength. The authority of God's infallible Word reveals God's truth and empowers our witness.)
4. Ask, What is an incarnational witness? (Living in flesh and blood a testimony of our faith so that our behavior and lifestyle are a witness to the people around us. Allowing people to see Jesus in us gives

159

credibility to a verbal witness.) Ask for responses to the activity on page 50.

5. Display and read the placard you prepared with the IMB's basic strategy. Ask, Why do you think the IMB considers missionary personnel its most valuable resource? (There are many methods and resources for doing missions, but it takes people to implement and use them. Jesus said to go because it is necessary for the gospel to be shared, and someone indwelled by God's Holy Spirit living among people as an incarnational witness gives credibility to the gospel.) Summarize that the IMB is a missionary-sending agency.

6. Write the following statistics on a dry-erase board and explain their meanings:
   • *1 missionary unit for every 1.6 million people*
   • *5,000 missionaries = 1 missionary for every 3,000 Southern Baptists*

   Ask, What percentage of Southern Baptists do you think God wants to call and use to reach the ends of the earth? Point out that 10 percent of Southern Baptists would be 1.6 million missionaries; only 1 percent would be 160,000 missionaries. Ask, Do you think Southern Baptists are capable of sending and supporting 1/10 of 1 percent, or 16,000 missionaries, instead of the current 5,000?

7. Ask for responses to the activity on page 51. Ask: Are any of these reasons justifiable? Why or why not?

8. Read Acts 13:2. Ask: How were Paul and Barnabas called as missionaries? Did they take the initiative, or did the church take the initiative in sending them? (The church) What was the church doing when it was impressed to send Paul and Barnabas? (Praying and fasting) What might happen to the calling and support of missionaries if believers prayed and fasted for unreached people groups and for a lost world? State, Prayer is an essential strategy for reaching the ends of the earth.

9. Ask whether any members have been on a prayerwalk while on a mission trip. If so, ask them to explain what they did and why.

10. Ask a member to read aloud Psalm 2:8. Link this promise with the earlier discussion of God's power as our essential resource in missions. Point out that we access that power through prayer. Ask if any members have regularly and systematically interceded in prayer for a particular nation or people group. Ask them to explain why they prayed for that particular nation or people group and what they prayed for. Ask, Why does God want us to pray for the nations? (We begin to share His burden for the lost and become responsive to what He wants us to do.)

11. Ask members to consider their responses to the final activity in day 3 (p. 54). Ask volunteers to share what the percentages reveal about the priority of missions in their prayers.

12. Divide members into three groups and give each group a large sheet of paper and a marker. Ask each group to brainstorm and list specific ways we can pray for missionaries. Allow a few minutes for

group work; then call for reports. (Ideas may include wisdom in planning their work and developing mission strategies; boldness in witnessing; hearts to be softened and responsive; a "man of peace" [Luke 10:6, NIV]—a person of influence to go before them and open doors of opportunity; the removal of barriers like religious prejudice, opposition, government and community restrictions, threats, and communication; personal and family needs; their walk with the Lord; protection and health; their children's education and social needs; relationships with colleagues; the pastors and lay evangelists with whom they work; the country served and government leaders; visas and work permits to be granted and renewed; protection from illness and danger; fluency in the language; an anointing of power and discernment; Satan's strongholds to be broken.)

13. Write the Web site address *www.imb.org* on a dry-erase board and state that this site provides resources for praying for and encouraging missionaries. Call on the member enlisted to report on some of the information on the Web site.

14. Call on the member enlisted to report on PRAYERPlus Partnerships. Ask whether members think their church could make this commitment.

15. Explain: Although God's power works through the personnel who go and through our prayers, believers and churches also need to provide the financial resources to reach the ends of the earth. Just as God blessed Abraham for him to be a blessing to the nations, God has blessed America, our church, and each of us in order to bless others through the gospel of Jesus Christ. Ask volunteers to explain the significance and purposes of the Cooperative Program and the Lottie Moon Christmas Offering® for International Missions. Supplement responses with the material in day 5.

16. Ask for responses to the activity on page 61. Correct members' ideas, if necessary, with the figures you discovered. Share the statistics in "Accountability for Resources," beginning on page 62. Ask: How much of a local church's receipts should be spent for missions beyond the support of its staff and local programs? How many international missionaries does your church have a part in supporting? (More than five thousand) Considering there are 43,000 churches and 16 million Southern Baptists, should our denomination be capable of supporting more than five thousand missionaries?

17. Ask volunteers to share ways this week's study has motivated them to do more personally in terms of praying, giving, or going. Ask, What can be done to influence and encourage our church to pray and give for missions?

18. Ask members to read week 4 and to complete the learning activities before the next session. Close by praying that members will obey whatever God leads them to do to reach the nations.

Session 4
Engaging the Whole World

Sessions Goals

After this session members will be able to—

- state why a church-planting movement is the most effective method for reaching a people group;
- identify ways various ministries and vocational skills can be used to gain access to restricted countries;
- distinguish between social ministries and evangelism;
- identify reasons certain people groups remain unreached;
- identify ways to finish the mission task.

Before the Session

1. Read week 4 and complete the activities.
2. Be prepared to show DVD segment 4.
3. Enlist a member to visit *www.imb.org,* read day 3, and report on the significance and purpose of the Southern Baptist World Hunger Fund.
4. Enlist two members to debate the ethics of using creative access to gain entry to countries that are closed to the gospel. Direct them to the topic "Creating Opportunities to Witness" in day 4.

During the Session

1. Show DVD segment 4.
2. Ask a volunteer to define *strategy.* (A plan or technique for accomplishing a goal) Ask: Why do missionaries and church partners need strategies for their work? (Keep attention and resources focused on kingdom growth) Why doesn't the IMB use a common global strategy? (The world is too diverse; cultures and languages are different; responsiveness varies.) Define *church-planting movement* and explain why this method is most effective in multiplying believers and churches in any people group. (Indigenous church planting is a flexible enough strategy to adapt to the needs of every culture or people group, so it can readily take root and grow.)
3. Explain that a church-planting strategy helps the IMB determine priorities. Ask volunteers to share responses to the activity near the bottom of page 67 and to give their rationales. (If all peoples are to have an opportunity to hear the gospel, a missionary or a witness must be assigned where people have not yet heard the gospel instead of where they may be responsive, where there are no other missionaries instead of where others are working, and where there are no churches instead of where churches are already established.) Call for responses to the activity on page 68. (The correct answer is 3.)
4. Use the examples in day 2 to explain how ministries and vocational skills can be used to gain access to restricted countries and provide platforms for the gospel.
5. Divide members into three groups and assign each group two of the roles in the

activity on page 71. Ask each group to discuss its examples and report on ways these ministries can be used to contribute to evangelism and church planting. Allow time to work; then call for reports. Ask whether members are involved in careers or have skills that could be used to bring people to saving faith in Jesus.

6. Point out the tension between emerging mission opportunities and established mission work. Ask for responses to the activity near the bottom of page 70.

7. Call on the member enlisted to report on the significance and purpose of the Southern Baptist World Hunger Fund. Note that 100 percent of the offering goes to alleviate suffering and hunger because Southern Baptists already provide for missionary support and administration through the Cooperative Program and the Lottie Moon Christmas Offering®. Ask whether any members have given to the World Hunger Fund.

8. Ask, What is the difference between social ministries and evangelism? (Social ministries provide humanitarian relief. Evangelism can meet not only physical needs but also spiritual needs through a relationship with Christ.) Call for responses to the true/false activity on page 74. (1. F, 2. F, 3. T, 4. F, 5. T, 6. T)

9. Ask a volunteer to define *creative access*. (Using vocational experience and skills to gain entry to a country and share the gospel) Introduce the two members enlisted to debate the ethics of using creative access to gain entry to countries that are closed to the gospel. The member with the opposing position should begin, followed by the advocate of this approach. After each side has been presented, read Acts 4:16-20 and emphasize the need to obey Jesus' command to share the gospel, regardless of the circumstances or the risk. Call for responses to the activity on page 78. (1. c, 2. b or d, 3. b or d, 4. a)

10. Define *Last Frontier* (see p. 77). Ask for responses to the activity at the top of page 79. (No conditions should be checked.)

11. Give members a moment to review day 5. Then ask: Why do some entire people groups remain unreached with the gospel? (Lack of missionaries, lack of vision by churches, oral cultures that cannot read the Bible or Christian literature, resistance by other religions and governments) What is the primary reason people remain unreached? (Believers are not obedient to the task and are not willing to go or provide more support for missionaries.)

12. Ask the group to identify things that could be done to finish the mission task and reach all peoples. Record these on a dry-erase board. Then ask members to name the ones your church could do. Place check marks beside these on the board. Finally, ask members to mentally identify what they could do personally.

13. Ask members to read week 5 and to complete the learning activities before the next session. Close with prayer.

Session 5
Church-Planting Movements

Session Goals

After this session members will be able to—

- identify characteristics of a New Testament church;
- define *church planting, church growth,* and *church-planting movement;*
- state why it is important for evangelistic efforts to result in local churches;
- identify elements that are essential to church planting;
- demonstrate an understanding of the term *indigenous church;*
- recognize ways church growth and evangelism can be hurt by subsidies to indigenous churches on the field.

Before the Session

1. Read week 5 and complete the activities.
2. Be prepared to show DVD segment 5.
3. Prepare a placard with the definition of *church* on page 87.
4. Prepare separate placards with the following terms and definitions:
   - *Church planting*
   - *Church growth*
   - *Church-planting movements*
   - *Efforts that bring new congregations into existence*
   - *A situation or an environment in which many churches are being planted and the number of churches is growing, primarily by addition*
   - *The rapid multiplication of new churches, primarily as churches start other churches*

5. Make copies of the following worksheet.

Mark each statement A for *agree* or D for *disagree.*

Financial subsidies from Western churches—

____ 1. create dependence and stifle local initiative;

____ 2. weaken faith by creating expectations that someone else will provide their needs;

____ 3. cause jealousy on the part of those who don't receive aid from abroad;

____ 4. promote the need for cooperation between local congregations;

____ 5. discourage a welfare mentality and encourage initiative;

____ 6. destroy a sense of ownership and the need to practice stewardship;

____ 7. create an improper concept of a church, based on a Western model;

____ 8. support the work and credibility of missionaries, who focus on spiritual ministry;

____ 9. often breed resentment when support is not continued indefinitely.

6. Enlist a member to describe the role of a missionary strategy coordinator in facilitating church-planting movements. Direct the member to the material in day 5.

During the Session

1. Ask a member to read aloud Acts 2:46-47. Ask volunteers to name characteristics of the New Testament church as you record these on a dry-erase board. Point to and read the definition of *church*. Ask, Is this definition consistent with the biblical pattern of a New Testament church?

2. Ask for responses to the activity on page 87. (Numbers 5 and 6 should be checked.)

3. Randomly display the placards you prepared. Ask a volunteer to try matching the terms with the definitions. Then ask the group whether the member matched them correctly. (*Church planting*: efforts that bring new congregations into existence. *Church growth*: a situation or an environment in which many churches are being planted and the number of churches is growing, primarily by addition. *Church-planting movements*: the rapid multiplication of new churches, primarily as churches start other churches.)

4. Show DVD segment 5. Explain that in America most churches have never started another church. Instead, churches are usually started independently. Emphasize that the gospel can be made accessible to all peoples only as local churches multiply to plant a witness in every community.

Point out the charts and statistics on church-planting movements in day 1.

5. Ask, Why is it important for evangelistic efforts to result in local churches? (New converts need to be part of a fellowship to nurture their growth. New believers' witness is stronger when they are part of a church fellowship. If churches do not result, an ongoing, expanded witness cannot be guaranteed.)

6. Ask a member to read 2 Timothy 2:2. Point out the four steps of training Paul outlined. (Paul taught Timothy, who was to pass on the teaching to faithful men, who were to teach others.) Explain that for indigenous local churches to multiply, church planting cannot depend on missionary church planters; rather, missionaries must train and equip local believers to carry out the work of ministry.

7. State that Paul's example reflects the importance of having local leaders rather than missionaries to lead the work. Read Acts 14:23 and explain that Paul had been in each city on his first missionary journey for only two or three weeks. Ask: Whom did he appoint or ordain in each church? (Elders/pastors) Where did these leaders come from? (New believers with leadership gifts in these new churches) Did he have trust and confidence primarily in the leaders' ability? (No, his confidence was in God, to whom he entrusted their leadership.)

8. Point out the four-step approach that missionaries use to plant churches and establish local leaders: modeling, assisting, watching, and leaving (see p. 89).

9. Ask, What does the term *indigenous church* mean? (Its biblical forms and functions are expressed in ways that are compatible with the local culture. It does not depend on outside resources and leaders to exist, grow, and multiply.)

10. What elements of American church life are indigenous to American culture? List responses on a dry-erase board. Which of these elements would not be indigenous to overseas cultures? On the board, place a check mark beside the elements that members name. Emphasize that Scripture and worship should always be in the heart language of the people and that the gospel must be communicated in the people's own cultural context.

11. Ask members to briefly review the topic "Common Factors in Successful Church Planting," beginning on page 91, and to name elements that are essential to church planting. Record responses on a dry-erase board. (A zeal for witnessing and sharing Jesus, reliance on God's Word for faith and practice, local lay pastors and indigenous leaders, worship in the heart language of the people, prayer, intentional efforts to start new churches) Summarize that an indigenous church must be self-supporting, self-governing, and self-propagating and must use worship forms that are consistent with the local culture.

12. Point out that the indigenous churches in the Book of Acts grew radically and spontaneously. Ask five members to read the following passages and to identify what they say about the New Testament churches' growth: Acts 2:46-47; Acts 5:14; Acts 5:42; Acts 9:31; Acts 16:5.

13. Explain that church growth and massive evangelistic harvest can be hurt by financial subsidies to indigenous churches on the mission field. Distribute copies of the agree/disagree worksheet you prepared and ask members to complete it. Then discuss the answers. (1. A, 2. A, 3. A, 4. D, 5. D, 6. A, 7. A, 8. D, 9. A) Emphasize the need to support mission work in a way that creates thriving indigenous congregations rather than dependency on direct Western support.

14. Call on the member enlisted to describe the role of a missionary strategy coordinator in facilitating church-planting movements. Emphasize that the strategy coordinator is not an authoritative leader but someone who facilitates and enables the team to effectively fulfill the planned mission strategies.

15. Call for responses to the final activity on page 98. (Only statements 3 and 7 should not be checked.)

16. Ask members to read week 6 and to complete the learning activities before the next session. Close with prayer.

SESSION 6
SENDING OUT THE CALLED

Session Goals

After this session members will be able to—

- define four qualifications for missionary service;
- identify long-term and short-term opportunities for mission service;
- state the importance of seven dimensions of missionary competencies;
- describe the relationship between the roles of the local church and the IMB in sending and supporting missionaries;
- name benefits of churches working cooperatively to support missions;
- identify factors that drive a missionary's passion and factors that prevent believers and churches from being passionate about missions.

Before the Session

1. Read week 6 and complete the activities.
2. Be prepared to show DVD segment 6.
3. Prepare four assignment slips with the following words or phrases:
   - *Piety*
   - *Zeal for the kingdom*
   - *Conviction of truth as held by Baptists*
   - *Talents for missionary service*
4. Enlist a member to report on types of long-term mission service with the IMB. Direct the member to the material in day 2.
5. Enlist a member to report on types of short-term mission service with the IMB. Direct the member to the material in day 3.
6. Order for all members copies of the brochure *Opportunities for Service* from International Mission Board; P.O. Box 6767; Richmond, VA 23230-0767.
7. Examine the diagram on page 110. Prepare a minilecture on the four phases of missionary orientation and the seven dimensions of missionary competencies, based on the related material in day 3.

During the Session

1. Show DVD segment 6.
2. Ask, Why is the IMB primarily a missionary-sending agency? (Jesus told us to go, and the church is mandated to send. Sending missionaries to plant their lives and witness in another culture is the most effective way to make the gospel known.) Call for responses to the activity on page 101. (An incarnational witness lives a flesh-and-blood testimony of our faith so that our behavior and lifestyle witness to people. Allowing people to see Jesus in us gives credibility to a verbal witness.)
3. Point out that historically, Southern Baptists have defined the qualifications for missionary service as piety, zeal for the kingdom, conviction of truth as held by Baptists, and talents for missionary service. Divide members into four groups and give each group one of the assignment slips you prepared. Ask each group to reach a consensus on the meaning

of its assigned qualification. After time for group work, call for reports.

- *Piety:* a heart for God, a meaningful prayer life, a disciplined quiet time and study of God's Word, a commitment to purity and holy living
- *Zeal for the kingdom:* a passion for people to come to faith in Jesus Christ, a commitment to Christ's lordship, obedience to God's will, a desire to see the gospel reach unevangelized people groups, and a desire for churches to be planted among the unreached and unchurched
- *Conviction of truth as held by Baptists:* personal doctrinal convictions that are consistent with Southern Baptist beliefs
- *Talents for missionary service:* experience indicating that someone has a commitment to ministry, is a personal witness, has gifts and abilities the Lord can use in mission service, and demonstrates flexibility to make cultural adjustments

Mention that other prerequisites include good physical and mental health; relational skills; and various educational requirements, depending on the category of service. Ask: Are these valid requirements for missionary appointment? Should other criteria be added?

4. Draw a vertical line on a dry-erase board to make two columns. Call on the member enlisted to report on categories of long-term mission service with the IMB. As the person reports, write the types of service in the left column under the heading *Long-Term Service: career*

missionaries, missionary associates, and missionary apprentices. Mention that many people refer to career missionaries as full-time missionaries when, in fact, all missionary personnel are full-time and are fully supported by Southern Baptists through the IMB. Point out that 75 to 80 percent of active missionary personnel are long-term missionaries, which means they are committed to serving indefinitely.

5. Call on the member enlisted to report on categories of short-term mission service. As the person reports, write the types of service in the right column under the heading *Short-Term Service: Journeyman, International Service Corps,* and *Masters Program.* Point out that the length of service for these categories is two or three years. Distribute copies of the brochure *Opportunities for Service.*

6. Ask, Why are long-term missionaries considered the most important category of service? (They can do more, nurture the work more effectively, learn the language, function in the culture more effectively, provide consistency of work over a period of time, and invest in discipling others and training leaders by building relationships over many years.)

7. Call attention to the graph on page 107. Ask the group to suggest reasons for the growth in short-term missionary appointments. (It coincides with ways God is at work in the world. Churches are more conscious of their mission task and are giving more emphasis to missions and

calling out missionaries. The increase in short-term volunteers has provided experiences through which God can impress other believers with a call to missions. World conditions signal a need for the gospel. More and more young people want to make a difference in the world. People are realizing ways diverse vocational skills can be used on the mission field.)

8. Call for responses to the activity on page 106. (All statements should be checked.)

9. Explain that the IMB requires training and experience prior to approval for missionary appointment, provides seven weeks of prefield training at the Missionary Learning Center, and offers continual on-the-field training. Refer members to the diagram on page 110. Present a minilecture on the four phases of missionary orientation and the seven dimensions of missionary competencies. Ask volunteers to state why they think each dimension is important.

10. Ask, What is the relationship between the roles of the local church and the IMB in sending and supporting missionaries? (The IMB facilitates the sending and support of missionaries, while churches equip, call, support, and maintain personal involvement with missionaries.)

11. Call for responses to the activity on page 112. (Mobilization and enlistment, orientation and training, coordinating travel and financial services, directing field strategies)

12. Reemphasize the role and importance of the Cooperative Program in providing coordinated financial support for Southern Baptist missionaries. Ask, What are the benefits of churches working cooperatively instead of independently to support missions? (Coordinated mission efforts, ability to support multiple missionaries more effectively, freedom for missionaries and churches to minister instead of raise money, a biblical plan that God has blessed, coordinated administration and training, logistical support for missionaries and their families)

13. Call for responses to the activity on page 113. (Items 1, 2, 3, 5, 6, and 7 should be checked.)

14. Use the ideas in day 5 to define the passion that motivates and drives missionaries. Ask members to name factors that drive a missionary's passion. List these in a column on the left of a dry-erase board. Then ask members to name factors that prevent believers and churches in the States from having the same passion about missions. List these in a column on the right of the dry-erase board. Ask, Are only missionaries called to a missions lifestyle? (No) Call for responses to the activity on page 116. Try to get a response in each area listed.

15. Ask members to read week 7 and to complete the learning activities before the next session. Close by praying that God will lead each member and each church to adopt a missions lifestyle so that we will have a heart and a commitment to extend God's kingdom to the ends of the earth.

SESSION 7
MAKING A GLOBAL IMPACT

Session Goals

After this session members will be able to—

- name essential skills for short-term mission volunteers;
- identify scenarios that have the greatest potential for evangelistic response;
- name three resources, besides career missionaries, for reaching the world;
- define *worldview*;
- identify ways to prepare for an effective cross-cultural witness;
- define *Acts 1:8 Challenge*;
- identify four mission fields for which churches are responsible;
- assess their church's willingness to be directly involved in missions.

Before the Session

1. Read week 7 and complete the activities.
2. Be prepared to show DVD segment 7.
3. Discover the number of short-term volunteers from your church who went on overseas mission projects last year, if any, or from your state.
4. Make a poster with these mission resources:
   - *Baptist partners around the world*
   - *Other evangelical believers, churches, and mission agencies*
   - *Short-term mission volunteers*
5. Prepare a placard with the definition of *worldview* on page 125.
6. Enlist a member to explain the concept of connecting with a missionary. Enlist another member to explain the concept of adopting a people group. Direct the members to the related material in day 4.
7. Make a placard with the definition of *Acts 1:8 Challenge* on page 132.

During the Session

1. Show DVD segment 7.
2. Ask whether any members have been on a short-term mission trip. Ask: Where did you go? What was the nature of your project? What did you accomplish? What difference did the experience make in your life? Was it worth the time and cost?
3. Explain that with five thousand international career missionaries around the world, Southern Baptists have only one missionary unit for approximately every 1.6 million people. It will take many more than that to reach the ends of the earth. One answer lies in short-term volunteer missions involvement. Point out that if each of the 43,000 Southern Baptist churches sent out a team of 5 volunteers just once a year, that would be more than 200,000 volunteers instead of the current level of about 30,000. Report the number of short-term volunteers from your church who went on overseas mission projects last year, if any, or from your state.
4. Ask for responses to the activity at the bottom of page 120. (Members should have checked numbers 4, 5, and 6.)

Emphasize that the most important qualification for being a mission volunteer is a desire to share God's love with people. Challenge members to consider going on a mission trip as often as God leads. Tell them not to wait until they feel they can afford to go but to trust God to provide the financial means.

5. State that volunteer mission work must be compatible with the strategies of missionaries on the field. Using day 2, describe the team structure that enables career missionaries to reach more people groups. Missionary teams are organized for long-range objectives, and their presence on the field enhances what volunteer teams do if joint planning occurs and field personnel are consulted and allowed to facilitate the project. Missionaries' involvement ensures better preparation and follow-up for short-term mission projects.

6. Ask, Is it better for the IMB to use personnel and resources to cultivate ripe harvest fields that readily respond to the gospel or to expand to unreached people groups, where the response may be slow? Ask for a show of hands to indicate agreement with each approach. Using the material in day 2, explain that our task to reach the whole world is a matter of balance and priority, not the exclusion of one method over the other. The IMB seeks to introduce the gospel to as many people groups as possible, knowing that indigenous believers and churches have the greatest potential to reach others. Missions is not a matter of winning as many people as possible but taking the gospel to all peoples so that everyone has an opportunity to hear and respond. A people group's responsiveness depends on its access to the gospel; a group cannot be considered unresponsive if it has never heard the gospel.

7. Write this sentence on a dry-erase board and ask a volunteer to explain its meaning: *The resources are in the harvest.* (People won to the Lord and churches started become resources to witness to others and start other churches rather than missionaries or volunteers from other countries supplying all of the resources. Those who respond to the gospel multiply the resources and potential to share the gospel.)

8. Call for responses to the activity at the bottom of page 123. (The greater potential response in each pair: 10 churches planting 100 new churches rather than 100 churches planting 10; 10 new churches with 30 members each rather than 2 churches with 200 members, because a more widespread witness is established in 10 locations; 50 churches reporting 1,000 baptisms is far more significant than 1,000 churches reporting 2,000 baptisms.)

9. State, Reaching the ends of the earth will never be accomplished solely by career missionaries. Ask, What are three other resources God is using to reach the world? (Baptist partners around the world; other evangelical believers, churches, and mission agencies; short-term mission volunteers) Show the poster you prepared.

10. Ask a volunteer to define *worldview.* After responses, show the placard you prepared. Explain that a worldview determines how someone fits into society and relates to the world. It determines social mores, behavior, values, and relationships. While Americans are very individualistic, people in other cultures are greatly influenced by cultural worldview. Their religious beliefs are shaped by generations of influence about how they relate to the spirit world.

11. Ask, Why is it important that people hear and understand the gospel in their own cultural context? (Meanings are filtered through their understanding and background, so they may not understand foreign religious concepts and assumptions.) Illustrate with examples from day 3.

12. Call for answers to the activity on page 128. (1. F, 2. T, 3. F, 4. T, 5. T) Discuss responses as needed.

13. Read the options in the activity at the bottom of page 127. State that all of these are valid ways a person can prepare for an effective cross-cultural witness.

14. Mention the trend toward direct, ongoing involvement by churches in missions. Introduce the member enlisted to explain the concept of connecting with a missionary. Ask, What are specific ways our church can enhance the work of a missionary and facilitate his or her reaching the people group? Record ideas on a dry-erase board.

15. Introduce the member enlisted to explain the concept of adopting a people group. Ask members to name specific ways their church could reach such a people group. Record ideas on a dry-erase board.

16. Ask a member to read Acts 1:8. Define *Acts 1:8 Challenge,* using the placard you prepared. Discuss what it means to be an Acts 1:8 church (see day 5). Write in a column on the left of a dry-erase board *Jerusalem, Judea, Samaria, Ends of the Earth.* Ask members to name components of their mission field that correspond to these. Record responses beside the words on the dry-erase board. (Jerusalem = community, Judea = region, Samaria = continent, ends of the earth = world) State that every church has a responsibility to each of these mission fields.

17. Further emphasize direct involvement in missions by asking members to scan "Partnerships Built on Relationships" on page 133 and to name the three levels of church involvement in missions. (Prayer, projects, partnership) Write the levels on a dry-erase board as they are named and discuss their meanings, as presented in day 5.

18. Call for responses to the activity at the bottom of page 134. (1. e, 2. a, 3. b, 4. f, 5. d, 6. c, 7. g, 8. h) Ask members to identify specific ways your church is carrying out its commitment to kingdom growth in these ways. Ask them to assess their church's willingness to become an Acts 1:8 church by being involved in ongoing partnerships to reach a lost world.

19. Ask members to read week 8 and to complete the learning activities before the next session. Close with prayer.

SESSION 8
REACHING THE ENDS OF THE EARTH

Session Goals

After this session members will be able to—
- describe the way God sees the world;
- define *kingdom partnership;*
- describe five levels of kingdom partnership;
- name people groups in their city or neighborhood and identify ways their church can reach them;
- assess their church's level of missions involvement and identify actions that would indicate a higher commitment;
- express personal commitments to involvement in kingdom growth.

Before the Session

1. Read week 8 and complete the activities.
2. Be prepared to show DVD segment 8.
3. Prepare a placard with the definition of *kingdom partnership: a cooperative effort among those who are committed to the authority of the Bible to fulfill the Great Commission and bring all peoples to saving faith in Jesus Christ.*
4. Draw a large version of the diagram on page 141 depicting the five levels of kingdom partnership.
5. Enlist a member to summarize the five levels of church involvement in global missions presented in day 4. Give the member the option of drawing a poster-size version of the diagram on page 148 or of simply referring to that page during the presentation.

During the Session

1. Show DVD segment 8. Reiterate Dr. Rankin's challenge that we should be well informed about mission strategy, the work of the IMB, how God is at work to extend His kingdom to the ends of the earth, and how each individual and church can be involved in fulfilling the Great Commission. However, information and awareness don't accomplish anything unless we also make a commitment to the mission task—as individual believers and as a church.
2. State: We must see the world as God sees it. Read Matthew 9:36. Ask, How does Jesus see a lost world? (He feels compassion because people are "weary and worn out, like sheep without a shepherd.")
3. Ask two members to read aloud Ephesians 4:28 and 1 John 3:17. Ask: What do these verses tell us to do? (Give to those in need) What is our motivation for giving? (God's love within us)
4. Ask two members to read aloud Isaiah 42:8 and Proverbs 16:18. Emphasize that a kingdom worldview means we are more concerned about God's glory and purpose than with getting credit or controlling what is done. A kingdom worldview enables us to cooperate with other kingdom partners to reach the ends of the earth.
5. Show the placard with the definition of *kingdom partnership.* Ask: What are the verbs in this definition? *(Are committed, fulfill, bring)*

What do they imply about the task of kingdom partners? (Active involvement) What is the result of the partnership? (Saving faith in Christ) Who are some kingdom partners with the IMB? (Other Southern Baptist entities, overseas Baptist churches and conventions, other evangelical mission agencies) Emphasize that Southern Baptists never compromise the truths of God's Word in forming partnerships with other groups.

6. Display the diagram you prepared showing the five levels of kingdom partnership (p. 141). Ask members to review the material in day 2 and to describe each of the five levels. Record key words on the diagram as the levels are described.

7. State that we don't have to go overseas to reach the nations and peoples of the world. Almost every people group in the world can be found in the United States, many within our own city and community. In going to the ends of the earth, we must not ignore those on our own doorstep. Ask members to name the nationalities, people groups, and religious adherents who are not native to America and live in their city or neighborhood. List these in a column on the left side of a dry-erase board. Ask, What is our church doing to share the gospel among these people groups? Ask the group to name ethnic groups in their city or state that represent cultures that are native to America or have lived here for generations. List these in a column on the right side of the dry-erase board. Draw

a bridge between the two columns and ask, What can we do to bridge the cultural and language gaps to befriend them and share the gospel?

8. Call on the member enlisted to summarize the five levels of church involvement in global missions presented in day 4. Ask members to identify their church's level of missions involvement and to give reasons for their assessment. Ask, What can our church do to move to the next level?

9. Read Matthew 24:14 and Acts 1:7-8. State that until Jesus returns, our focus is to be on the task He left for us to do—evangelizing the world. Ask, What would happen if our church committed itself to extend God's kingdom to the ends of the earth? (Possible responses: Missionaries would be called out of our church. Church members would be better stewards and give more generously. We would be more effective in local evangelistic efforts. God would bless and prosper our local programs. We would experience a new anointing of God's power. We would get to be involved in reaching unreached people groups with the gospel.)

10. Refer members to the activity on page 152. Ask volunteers to share what commitment(s) God is leading them to make in order to be personally involved in kingdom growth.

11. Close by allowing volunteers to offer prayers of commitment and to request God's guidance in fulfilling His mission.

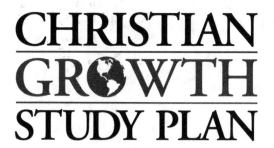

CHRISTIAN GROWTH STUDY PLAN

In the Christian Growth Study Plan *To the Ends of the Earth* is a resource for course credit in the subject area Missions in the Christian Growth category of diploma plans. To receive credit, read the book; complete the learning activities; attend group sessions; show your work to your pastor, a staff member, or a church leader; then complete the form. This page may be duplicated. Send the completed form to:

Christian Growth Study Plan
One LifeWay Plaza; Nashville, TN 37234-0117
Fax (615) 251-5067; e-mail *cgspnet@lifeway.com*
For information about the Christian Growth Study Plan, refer to the current *Christian Growth Study Plan Catalog,* located online at *www.lifeway.com/cgsp.* If you do not have access to the Internet, contact the Christian Growth Study Plan office, (800) 968-5519, for the specific plan you need.

To the Ends of the Earth
COURSE NUMBER: CG-1199

PARTICIPANT INFORMATION

Social Security Number (USA ONLY-optional)	Personal CGSP Number*	Date of Birth (MONTH, DAY, YEAR)

Name (First, Middle, Last)		Home Phone

Address (Street, Route, or P.O. Box)	City, State, or Province	Zip/Postal Code

Email Address for CGSP use

Please check appropriate box: ❑ Resource purchased by church ❑ Resource purchased by self ❑ Other

CHURCH INFORMATION

Church Name

Address (Street, Route, or P.O. Box)	City, State, or Province	Zip/Postal Code

CHANGE REQUEST ONLY

☐ Former Name

☐ Former Address	City, State, or Province	Zip/Postal Code

☐ Former Church	City, State, or Province	Zip/Postal Code

Signature of Pastor, Conference Leader, or Other Church Leader	Date

*New participants are requested but not required to give SS# and date of birth. Existing participants, please give CGSP# when using SS# for the first time. Thereafter, only one ID# is required. **Mail to:** Christian Growth Study Plan, One LifeWay Plaza, Nashville, TN 37234-0117. Fax: (615)251-5067.

Revised 4-05

Reaching the Ends of the Earth:
Hear the Call, Accept the Challenge

These resources will ignite your passion for the lost and will help you discover your role in God's global redemptive plan.

TO THE ENDS OF THE EARTH *by Jerry Rankin*

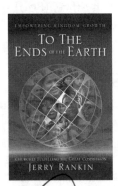

The trade-book edition of this workbook study provides an awareness of how God is at work throughout the world, an understanding of the strategy and work of the International Mission Board, and ideas for owning and participating in the mission task. Use this book to share with others the urgent need to reach a lost world for Christ.

Softcover Book Item 0-8054-4425-4

BASIC TRAINING FOR MISSION TEAMS
by Jerry Rankin & Phyllis Tadlock

This seven-session group study in the Impact Your World series equips mission teams for successful mission trips. It guides participants to explore the worldview and culture of their destination, to saturate their planning in the Word and in prayer, to plan the best use of their time, and to formulate strategies for maximum impact.

Member Book Provides seven weeks of study and preparation tools. Item 1-4158-3543-8

Leader DVD/CD-ROM Pack Includes DVD and CD-ROM with numerous worksheets and planning tools. Item 1-4158-2606-4

To order, call (800) 448-8032, go to *www.lifewaystores.com*, or visit the LifeWay Christian Store serving you.